THE
SUPER HANDYMAN'S
BIG BIKE BOOK

THE SUPER HANDYMAN'S

BIG

BIKE

BOOK

by *Al Carrell*
"THE SUPER HANDYMAN"

PRENTICE-HALL, INC., *Englewood Cliffs, New Jersey*

The Super Handyman's Big Bike Book by Al Carrell
Copyright © 1973 by King Features Syndicate, Inc.
All rights reserved. No part of this book may be
reproduced in any form or by any means, except
for the inclusion of brief quotations in a review,
without permission in writing from the publisher.
Printed in the United States of America
Prentice-Hall International, Inc., London
Prentice-Hall of Australia, Pty. Ltd., North Sydney
Prentice-Hall of Canada, Ltd., Toronto
Prentice-Hall of India Private Ltd., New Delhi
Prentice-Hall of Japan, Inc., Tokyo

Library of Congress Cataloging in Publication Data
Carrell, Al.
  The super handyman's big bike book.

  1. Bicycles and tricycles—Maintenance and repair.
I. Title.
TL430.C37   629.28'7'72   72–13944
ISBN 0-13-875989-8 (pbk)
10 9 8 7 6 5 4 3

Contents

THE
SUPER HANDYMAN'S
BIG BIKE BOOK

1

Introduction—How to Use This Book

As recently as 1965, in an article in the July 25 issue of *Engineering,* the death knell of the bicycle was tolled. "The cycle industry has been one of the casualties of the rise in living standards." Adios, bicycles! And yet, an industry leader who's a little on the conservative side says there'll be over 10 million bikes to "roll" off the assembly line this year. He also says there'll be a 10 percent increase in production next year. All industries should suffer such a death!

How did it all start? The first crude form of bike was called the *célérifère.* It consisted of a padded bar to sit on and a wheel on each end. Its go-power came from the rider's feet pushing along the ground. It lacked one element that made it less than a winner —the front wheel was fixed, and therefore the machine could not be steered. There is much controversy over who the inventor actually was. The date has been set at around 1790.

Along about 1816, one cycler got tired running into things and came up with a steering mechanism.

During the next fifty years, a bit of chrome was added here and a new paint scheme there, and a foxtail attached yonder. In about 1860, though, the pedal was attached to the bike—or rather two pedals.

The machine was first given the name "bicycle" in about 1868. Until then it had been called by many names, some of which are printable—such as hobby-horse, dandy horse, swift walker, high wheeler, ordinary, bone shaker, velocipede, and penny-farthing.

The bike began to resemble today's bicycles in 1885 when the so-called safety bicycle was introduced. It had brakes, rubber tires, and chain drive, and both wheels were the same size.

Since that time most of the advances have been in the form of improvements—until just recently, when it became possible to buy bikes on easy terms. The finance companies and banks ask that you read this book and keep their property in good shape. (Speaking of banks, not long ago a loan bandit stuck up a big city bank and got away with $7,300—on a 10-speed.)

How did this almost two-hundred-year-old contraption make such a comeback? I feel the very thing that *Engineering* said was killing the cycle industry caused the rebirth. The "rise in living standard" saw everyone with a car and more leisure time. The natural thing to do was to go somewhere on the free time, and then came the problem—how to get on the freeway. For those who made it, it was bumper-to-bumper all the way.

So all at once, millions of people decided to do their own thing for the planet, and at the same time do something nice for their very own bodies. The bicycle offered a way to spend leisure time without polluting the air, and at the same time build a body that would be better looking and possibly last longer. Besides, when you got where you were going, you didn't have to worry about a parking space.

There are now several books out on cycling. Some cover the history of cycling, biking for health, pedaling for ecology, bicycle racing, and tours you can take on your bike. While we may mention some of that good stuff, this book is on maintenance and repair. The cycler whose machine is working properly at all times is a happy soul. He'll enjoy riding, and thus stay healthy and help others stay healthy by not polluting the air. He'll decide for himself about tours and racing.

Hopefully, you'll find taking care of your bike such a snap that if anything does go wrong, you won't be afraid to tackle it. In short, you'll become a Super Cycler!

Since the idea behind this book is to carry you through each step of a repair or maintenance job, we'll start with the step-by-step method of using the book.

1A-1. Pay for the book.

1A-2. Read the Glossary (Chapter 2). Then when we speak "bike-talk," you'll know what we're talking about.

1A-3. Next, read the "General Rules of Thumb" (Chapter 7). These are things that you must know and remember.

1A-4. Leaf through the book to see what subjects are covered and *how* they're covered. Step-by-step procedures are identified by chapter number and a capital letter. Thus, the first step-by-step procedure in Chapter 8 is Procedure 8A, steps 1, 2, and 3. Simple, isn't it?

1A-5. Pick out the parts that apply to your bike and skim these. If a particular assembly or part reads like Greek to you, sit by your bike while you read about that part. Compare your bike with the drawings. You'll begin to see just where everything falls in place—and how to put it back together.

1A-6. Now, go to Chapter 5. Maintenance checklist. Read every word of it. Even if there's not one single thing wrong with your bike, start on the maintenance steps *today!*

1A-7. When you have a problem with your bike, go to the Troubleshooting Section of Chapter 5 and see if it won't direct you to the exact page. If it doesn't, go to the chapter that applies —you'll find the key. Then just go through the easy-to-follow steps to get it fixed. Read carefully, do what I tell you, be patient, and above all—*have confidence!*

If you lack faith in your bike-fixing abilities, keep in mind that not everyone who repairs bicycles is a mechanical whiz. Chances are that at least one of the "mechanics" at the neighborhood bike shop is a part-time employee who's a junior in high school and learned how last week. If he can learn it—so can you!

Once you get going, your confidence will grow, and what used to be a frightening repair job will become fun tinkering.

Since almost every country in the world has at least one bicycle manufacturer, it's impossible to include every make and model of brakes, gears, and other assemblies in a book of this modest price. However, the parts covered are typical. If we didn't hit yours exactly, pick out the one closest to yours, and by following the steps, you'll figure out how to do the same thing on your model. After all, you were smart enough to buy this book in the first place.

2

Glossary of
Bike Terms

Unlike most books, this one has its glossary right here at the beginning. After all, if you learn what these words mean, you'll better understand what we're talking about later on. If you don't have total recall, it's OK to flip back to this section to look up a word when you're stumped.

Also, there is a drawing of a bike at the end of this glossary which may help you to see where some of these parts are situated.

Allen Wrench: Also known as a *hex wrench* or *hex key*. The hex tip fits in a hex-shaped slot in an Allen screw or bolt.

All-Rounder: Handlebars of the old conventional type that aren't curved under.

Axle: The pin, shaft, or bar around which something turns. In addition to the conventional wheel-axle relationship, there are parts referred to as axles in other assemblies on some bikes.

Balloon Tire: Those fat jobs found on many coaster-brake bikes; a low-pressure tire.

Banana Seat. Also known as a *stingray seat*. It looks a lot more like a banana than a stingray. It's a long saddle with a rear brace. Very popular with the younger set.

Bar Plug: An end plug for tape-wrapped handlebars.

Beads: See **Clinchers.**

Binder Bolt: The nut-and-bolt assembly that goes through the clamp that holds the handlebar to the gooseneck.

Bottom Bracket: The short cylinder through which the crank assembly fits.

Brake Pads: The rubber shoes found on caliper brakes.

Cable: Twisted wire that goes to caliper brakes or derailleurs.

Cage: The term given to the arms that hold the small wheels or rollers of the rear derailleur.

Caliper Brakes: Hand brakes.

Center Pulls: A hand-brake system.

Chain Stays: The arms of the frame running from the bottom bracket to the rear of the bike. The rear wheel rides between them.

Chainwheel: The front sprocket or sprockets.

Clinchers: Tires that have a separate tube. The tire is held to the rim by a bead that fits in the lip of the rim when the tire is inflated. The bead is formed by a wire encased in the casing. They are also called *wire-ons*.

Coaster Brakes: Rear wheel foot-activated brakes with the works in the rear hub.

Cone: A threaded part that is sometimes cone-shaped. It usually fits next to a bearing and is used for adjusting.

Cotter Pin: A tapered part that holds the crank to the bottom bracket axle on some crank assemblies.

Crank: The kind of bike repairman to avoid. Also, the assembly that holds the pedals and chainwheel. It fits through and on either side of the bottom bracket. Sometimes called *crankset*.

Cyclometer: Mileage gauge.

6

Derailleur: The external gear unit that moves (derails) the chain from one sprocket to another. Both front and rear units are called derailleurs.

Dishing: The flattened effect on the right side of a rear wheel on a derailleur-equipped bicycle. The spokes on the right side are tighter than the others, so as to pull the wheel over to center over the entire axle instead of just the hub.

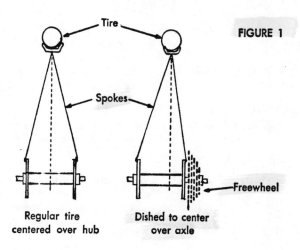

Regular tire
centered over hub

Dished to center
over axle

FIGURE 1

Down Tube: The part of the frame running from the head tube down to the bottom bracket.

Drop Outs: Slots in the frame and fork into which the wheel axles fit.

Dust Cap: Any number of shaped cups that enclose a part or an assembly to keep out dust and grime.

Fork Crown: The flat part of the fork from which the two arms come down and the fork tube sticks up.

Freewheel: The cluster of sprockets on the rear of a derailleur-equipped bicycle. The name has nothing to do with the price.

#@%&*¢÷?+½#: A bike term muttered or yelled when the repair work isn't going according to the book.

Gooseneck: See **Stem**.

Headset: The workings that hold the fork in the frame.

Head Tube: The short tube at the front of the frame in which fork and stem join together. This is where the headset is housed.

Hub: The wheel unit that houses the axle assembly and to which the spokes are attached.

Jockey Wheel: Also called the *jockey roller*. This is the top roller in the rear derailleur cage that moves the chain from one rear sprocket to another.

Left-Hand Threads: Those that need to be turned counterclockwise to tighten and clockwise to loosen, which is opposite to the norm.

Metric Wrenches: Almost every country in the world except the United States uses the metric system in measuring things. Nuts and bolts are measured in terms of millimeters (mm) instead of fractions of an inch. Metric wrenches are needed for these parts.

Mudguards: Fenders.

Multispeed Hubs: Geared bikes in which the gear mechanism is located in the rear hub.

Pawls: A pivoted arm that catches on teeth to prevent movement.

Planet Gear: A gear-toothed wheel that revolves around and meshes with a center or *sun gear*.

Power Train: The "go" system which includes the pedals, sprockets, and chain and the gears, if any.

Quick Release: A spring-held hand lever that releases a part or an assembly with a flick of a finger instead of having to turn a nut.

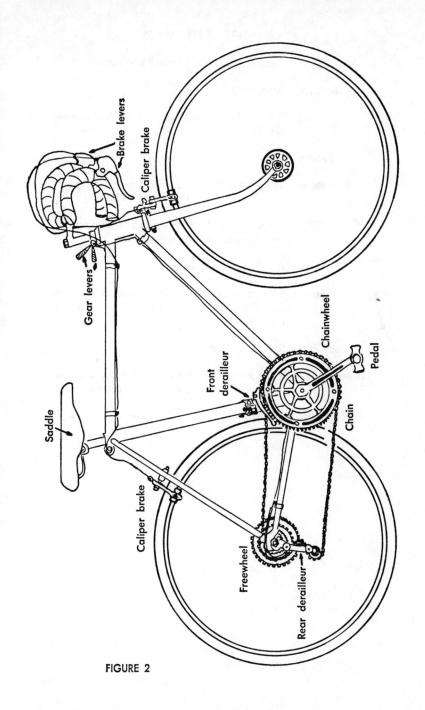

Brake levers

Caliper brake

Gear levers

Chainwheel

Pedal

Front
derailleur

Saddle

Chain

Caliper brake

Freewheel

Rear derailleur

FIGURE 2

Race: The track or groove in which ball bearings run.

Rattrap: All-metal pedals.

Rim: The metal ring to which spokes attach and on which the tire fits.

Saddle: Seat.

Seat Stays: The arms of the frame running from the top of the seat tube down to where the rear wheel fits.

Seat Tube: The part of the frame into which the seat post fits. It goes down to the bottom bracket.

Shim: A part that fills space.

Stem: The curved or angled part in which the handlebars are held. The other end is held in the fork tube inside the head tube.

Sun Gear: See **Planet Gear.**

Tension Roller: The bottom wheel in the rear derailleur cage that adjusts chain tension as gears are changed.

Tubes: The bars that comprise the frame.

Wired-Ons: See **Clinchers.**

3

Selecting,
Fitting,
and Assembling

_____ **If you're buying a bike**

We believe that most people who buy, borrow, or
steal this book will already own a bicycle. However,
you may be faced with buying another for some other
member of your family—or you may wish to up-
grade and get a bike with more or better gears.

I'm not going to tell you what make of bicycle
to buy. There are many good ones, made here in the
U.S. and in many foreign countries. The type of bike
you buy depends on what you'll be using it for. If it's
for a kid, get a sturdy inexpensive one that's in
style—popular with the kids. Be prepared to trade
it off next year when the child outgrows it, or when
a new style comes in.

If you're going to do much riding at all, I do
recommend a bike with gears. How many gears is
largely a matter of what you want from your bike
and what you wish to spend. Another consideration
is the weight of the bike. A heavy bike gets to be a
lot heavier when you have very far to go.

If you've never had a bike with the turned under
handlebars and skinny little seat, you probably think
it looks awfully uncomfortable. Try it! You'll like it!
Not at first, but after you use it and get used to it,
you will. That crouched-over position actually allows
you to use different muscles, so you don't tire so
quickly. The skinny saddle is all that's needed, since
the crouched-over position shifts some of your weight
off the seat and onto the handlebars. A wide seat

11

doesn't allow for free thigh movement. It takes some getting used to, but it's worth it if you do much riding.

Whether you're going to buy a new bicycle or shop for a bargain on a used one, the most important consideration is size. Maybe you never thought about bikes having sizes—other than "kids" and "adults"— but they do. The wrong-sized machine can make riding become sheer torture. It can give you a near hernia, almost break your back, make it impossible to pedal uphill, and actually be dangerous.

The place to make sure your bike fits is the frame. If the frame is right, most of the other things are easily adjusted to fit you.

Don't confuse frame size with wheel size. A bike with 27″ wheels can have a 20″ frame or a 25″ frame. Those inches and even half-inches make a difference. But what does frame size mean?

The distance in inches from the seat lug down the seat tube to the center of the bottom bracket is the frame size. (See Figure 3.) If the frame is your correct size, it will allow you to stand barefoot astraddle the bike easily and comfortably. Women who prefer the open frame style will find that the best frame size is about nine or ten inches less than their inseam measures barefooted. I would suggest you measure at home, but don't hesitate to get barefooted at the bike shop—they're used to it.

After you determine the correct size frame, you will want to adjust several other parts to your body. But you must be sure that there is enough length in the seat post and handlebar stem to allow these two parts to be adjusted to you. Usually, after you find the best size frame for you, you won't have any other problems unless you have unusually long or short arms or legs.

The seat, or saddle as bike purists call it, should allow you to stretch your leg out to its full length with the ball of your foot at a slight angle when the pedals are at the position shown. A good way to set this is to have a friend hold the bike upright while you test the seat setting.

It is important that the setting be right to begin with because your body will adjust to the setting, and

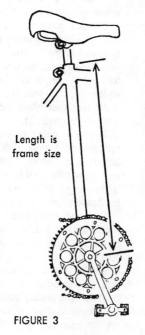

Length is frame size

FIGURE 3

if it's not right, you'll adjust to something less than the most efficient use of your muscles. If you get a bike that fits your body, your needs, and your pocketbook, you'll get a lot more enjoyment out of cycling.

Assembly

If a new bike is not put together correctly when you buy it, you're in for trouble. The boo-boos either prevent the proper operation or eventually cause something to wear out before its time.

Most bike shops don't sell their wares knocked down in the carton for you to worry about. However, the great American custom of "buying it wholesale"—plus the large number of hardware, department, and discount stores with bicycles to sell—means lots of folks pick out the machine of their choice and then get a box of parts.

"Don't panic . . . the instructions are in the carton," the salesman tells you. I'd advise you to panic. The assembly is not an impossible task, however, and you'll learn a lot about your bike, but gather up the proper tools and allot plenty of time.

> RULE OF THUMB: *If the instructions say it will take an hour to assemble, double the time and add a minute for every year old you are.*

Hopefully, the instructions will be in English! However, if your bicycle is foreign-made, the translation will have been made by a guy who learned English in high school. (How fluently do you speak the foreign language *you* took in high school?)

The best suggestion I have is to follow the order of assembly in the instructions, and if you get stuck, refer to the part of this book that covers the assembly that's got you buffaloed.

Next, if at all possible, have an accomplice. Four hands are better than two.

After it's all together, resist the urge to leap on and pedal off into the sunset until *all* adjustments have been made—including correct air pressure in the tires.

> **RULE** OF **THUMB:** *After using any new bike for a few days—whether you assembled it or not—check to see if all the nuts and bolts are still tight, and if everything is still in adjustment.*

4

Bike Safety

In the event of a confrontation with a car, a tree, or a brick wall, the average bicycle offers very little protection for the rider. Therefore, it behooves the Super Cycler to avoid an accident.

The first step to safety is to have a safe machine. *Everything* must be working properly. The brakes, steering, gears, wheels, and whatever else you've got must do their thing for safety's sake. The use of the maintenance chart in Chapter 5, plus common sense, will assure everything staying A-OK.

The proper fit is also important to your safety, and both seat and handlebars must be on good and tight as well as positioned to fit.

Local ordinances probably require lights and reflectors for night cyclers. Even if there are no local ordinances, you don't have to be a Phi Beta Kappa to know you should be visible at night. The more reflectors you have on you and your bike, the better off you are.

Here are a few ideas the readers of my column have come up with for extra visibility:

"Our son has a morning paper route which means he's out on his bike while it's still dark. To make it easier for any early motorists to spot him, I put reflector tape strips all around the bottoms of his sneakers. A headlight would make the moving reflector strips really jump out at the motorist." Not a bad way to make yourself more visible!

Another reader suggested: "I have wrapped a small tab of reflector tape around each spoke on

my daughter's bike so she'll be easily seen at night.
The headlight and taillight take care of the front
and back, and the spinning reflector bands take care
of the sides."

Still another came up with the idea of reflector
tape on his son's belt. The idea is that children
should be seen and not hit. Not a bad idea for all
cyclers.

SAFETY RULES OF THUMB—Make sure your bike is in proper
working order: brakes, tires, gears, lights, etc.

Know and observe all traffic rules—generally, cyclers have to
follow the same rules as motorists, with a few extras.

Keep as far to the right as practical.

If there are two or more bikers, ride single file.

Have a signaling device—horn or bell—positioned for easy
access. (Read Chapter 16.)

Have lights and reflectors for night riding. (More Chapter 16.)

Avoid sidewalks . . . some communities don't allow it anyway.

Give pedestrians the right-of-way.

Be alert to parked cars. They may pull out, a door may open
suddenly, or a child or other small person may be lurking out
of sight ready to step into your path.

Don't carry passengers! Lots of folks tote babies properly attached to their bike or back. I've done it, but it's safer if you
can avoid it.

16

Don't carry bulky packages that obstruct your view or impair your control of the bike.

Never hitch a ride.

Confine racing, acrobatics, and other suicide attempts to non-traffic areas.

Don't weave in and out of traffic, even if the traffic is light. Ride in a straight line.

Use the proper hand signals for turning or stopping. They're the same as those for motorists (See Figure 4).

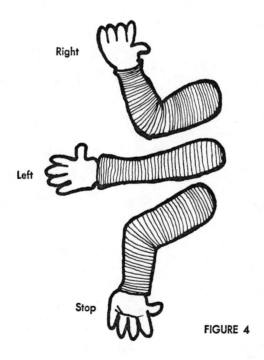

Right

Left

Stop

FIGURE 4

Remember that even though you have the right-of-way, if you are challenged by a 5,000-lb. Cadillac (or even a Bug) you can be dead right.

5
Checklist—
Maintenance
and Troubleshooting

To keep your bicycle operating at its peak requires TLC. Yes, that means Tender Loving Care, but it also means Tightening, Lubricating, and Cleaning.

The charts in this chapter are your guide to TLC for your bike. Over and above these tightening, lubing, and cleaning functions, always talk nicely to your bike and occasionally give it a pat on the fender to show you care. TLC can mean you don't have to use this book quite as often.

TLC MAINTENANCE CHART

WHEN TO CHECK	BIKE PART TO CHECK	WHAT TO DO TO IT
DAILY	THE ENTIRE	As you ride, make sure to try all gears, brakes, and accessories, and as you ride along, listen for any sign of something that is working differently and thus making a funny noise. (Also listen for trucks.)
WEEKLY	TIRES	Check pressure. Proper pressure should be stamped on tires. If not, look at the chart in Chapter 10.
	LIGHTS AND REFLECTORS	Be sure lights are bright and reflectors are positioned properly.
	THE ENTIRE	Clean your bike with a damp rag to remove dust. Wipe dry.
MONTHLY	THE ENTIRE	Polish all metal (except rims on bikes with caliper brakes—brake shoes won't grab slick rims).
	THE ENTIRE	Check all nuts and bolts to be sure they are properly tightened.
	TIRES	Hand inspect for cuts and bruises.
	CHAIN	Lubricate and check for proper tension. (Chapter 14.)
	GEARS—MULTISPEED HUBS	Lubricate hub and check adjustment. (Chapter 15.)
	GEARS-DERAILLEUR	Adjust front and rear units. Lubricate. (Chapter 15.)
	GEAR LEVERS	Adjust if needed. (Chapter 15.)

	BRAKES-COASTER	Lubricate hubs. (Chapter 12.)
	BRAKES-CALIPER	Check cable tension. See that shoes touch rims properly. Lubricate pivot points. (Chapter 12.)
	HEADSET	Check turning, tightness, and lubrication. (Chapter 11.)
	HANDLEBARS	Check tightness. Inspect wrap or grip. If on child's bike, keep pace with growth by adjusting. (Chapter 9.)
	SPROCKETS—CHAINWHEELS AND FREEWHEELS	Play dentist and check the teeth for wear or damage.
	WHEELS	Check alignment and position on frame or fork. Inspect rims for dents or other damage.
	SADDLE	Make sure the seat is on straight and tight. Clean the cover: if leather, use saddle soap; if mink, send out to furrier. If on a child's bicycle, adjust for growth.
SEMIANNUALLY	VARIOUS	Lubricate bearings in hubs, cranks, headset, etc.
	CHAIN	Remove, clean, and lubricate. (Chapter 14.)
	TOOLS	Check to be sure all are in good shape. Rub metal with a light coat of oil.
RULE OF THUMB:		'Tis better to use the wrong lubricant than none at all—just do it over the right way as soon as you can.

TROUBLESHOOTER'S QUICK-DRAW CHART

PART	WHAT'S WRONG WITH IT
SEATS	Side-to-side play 35-36 Up-and-down play 36 Seat too high or too low 35-36 Seat droops, sags, or has lumps 36-37 Cover dirty, torn, or frayed 36-37
HANDLEBARS	Bars are loose 38-39 Grip lost 42-43 Tape goofed 40-42 Stiff steering 73 Bars aren't positioned right 38-39 Loose steering 73
TIRES, WHEELS, AND SPOKES	Flat (sew-up tire) 50-52 Flat (clincher type) 46-47 Slow leaks 48 Uneven wear 54-56, 66-67 Front wheel wobbles 54 Rear wheel wobbles 54-56 Spoke broke 56-58 Loose spoke 56-63 Rim bent 58-63 Wheel rubs 54-56, 66-67 Wheel turns tight 66-67
FRAMES AND FORKS	Fork bent 71 Frame bent 68-70 Paint chipped 70
BRAKES	Coaster brakes grab 76-84 Wheel slips with coaster brakes 76-84 Noise inside coaster brake hub 76-84 Brakes squeal (coaster) 76-84 Brakes squeal (caliper) 85-86 Brake shoes rub tire 92 Brake cable breaks often 86-93 Lever sticks 87 Lever rattles 86 Lever loose on handlebar 86 Caliper brake sticks 86-93 Need new cable 93 Cable housing shot 93 Caliper brake shoes shot or crooked 92-93

TROUBLESHOOTER'S QUICK-DRAW CHART (*continued*)

PART	WHAT'S WRONG WITH IT
PEDALS	Pedal growls 98 Pedal loose 98 Pedal won't spin 98 Need new pedals 94-98 Pedal bent 94-98
SPROCKETS AND CRANKS	Teeth bent 99 Front sprocket wobbles 106 Crank loose 99 Crank hits something 99-103 Growls come forth as crank turns 106-109
CHAINS	Chain jumps off front sprocket 115-117 Chain jumps off rear sprocket 115-117 Chain hits something 119 Something caught in chain 119 Broken chain 113-114 Chain too loose 115 Chain makes funny noises 119
GEARS—MULTI-SPEED HUBS	Noise in hub 122 Gears shift on their own 122-123 Gears won't shift at all 122-123 No low gear 122-123 Gears feel as if they are slipping 122-123 Cable comes off 122-123 Hard to shift 122-123 Shifter control broken 140 Cable breaks 145
GEARS—DERAILLEUR	Chain won't transfer on front sprockets 147 Chain won't move on rear sprockets 147 Control lever moves by itself 147 Control lever won't move at all or is quite difficult 145 Cable breaks 146 Gears slow to change after lever is moved 147 Front cage hits something 155 Rear changer bent 147 Noise in rear changer when shift made 147

6

Tools, Parts, and Maintenance Racks

Tools you will need
and a few that would be nice to have

There is a good possibility that you'll have enough tools around the house to do many of the repair and maintenance chores. When we start talking about the actual work, we will mention all the tools that can be used for the task. If you don't have some of the more specialized tools, figure out the best substitute. But, don't botch up your bike by trying to use a tool that is totally wrong for the job.

Pliers • The home handyman will know that pliers are for gripping and should not be used instead of the proper wrench. However, the proper wrench is usually in the trunk of the car or has been borrowed by a neighbor. It's a lot easier to find the pliers. Be careful or you'll chew up the nut. If it's a metric nut, be particularly careful, as they aren't so easy to come by.

FIGURE 6

Adjustable End Wrench • A medium-sized one will take up the gap in your wrench supply. This is a lot better on nuts than a pair of pliers.

FIGURE 7

Open End and Box Wrenches • If you have an American-made bike with derailleurs, you'll find that you will need both regular and metric wrenches. The patents on the most popular derailleurs are foreign-held. Hence, American manufacturers will make most of the bike and have to order foreign-made parts. These wrenches usually come in sets. A set of regular wrenches from ⅜″ up to ¾″ and metrics from 6 mm to 16 mm will all find use. British bikes will require Whitworth wrenches instead of the regular set. They too will require metric tools for the derailleurs.

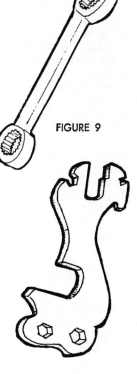

FIGURE 9

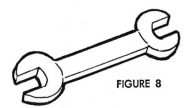

FIGURE 8

All-Purpose Wrenches • There are several different so-called all-purpose wrenches on the market. Some are designed to fit all the nuts and bolts on a particular kind of bike. They are handy for carrying because there's only one tool to worry about. They are nowhere near as good to work with as a set of tools. There isn't as much leverage, and they aren't as comfortable. Some manufacturers include such a tool when you buy the bike.

25

FIGURE 10

Cable Clipper • A good pair of wire clippers will do the job. If you have to buy some, I think the side cutter kind is better for bike cables than the end cutters. A good pair will cut down on your grief.

FIGURE 11

Tire Iron • This little tool is one you'll have to buy. Whatever you come up with as a substitute from the tool box won't work.

Tire Repair Kit • Get the kind that will enable you to fix a flat on your bike. Don't get a sew-up kit if you don't have sew-up tires. Makes sense, doesn't it?

Screwdriver • That one you have in the kitchen drawer is fine.

FIGURE 12

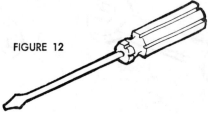

Tire Gauge • Be sure the one you get reads as high as your tires should be inflated.

Spoke Wrench • Here again you'll not be able to find a substitute, but they only cost pennies. Get the right gauge.

26

FIGURE 13

Chain Rivet Extractor • See Chapter 14 to find out if your chain requires one.

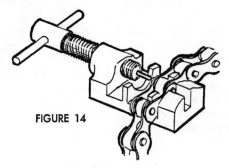

FIGURE 14

Freewheel Remover Nut • You'll find out about freewheels in Chapter 13. Believe me, this doesn't refer to the price.

FIGURE 15

Maintenance Rack • Take your choice later in this Chapter.

Allen Wrenches • Metric jobs are a big help for some derailleurs, as you'll learn later on.

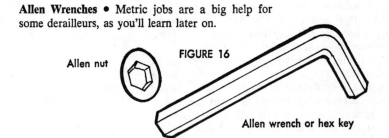

FIGURE 16

Allen nut

Allen wrench or hex key

Brake Arm Squeezer • A third hand if you have caliper brakes. Available only at bike shops.

FIGURE 17

Third hand—brake tool

Beyond this, dear friend, you are getting into the realm of the repair shop. Such things as rim truers, frame stretchers, and fork formers are going to require an investment that makes it impractical for the occasional user to purchase.

Lubricants

There are two basic types you should have—a lightweight machine oil and a lightweight grease. There are lots of brands of each type that are good, available at hardware stores as well as bike shops. (Generally, you'll pay a few cents more at the bike shop.) Also, there are spray lubes that are great. When other lubricants are better, we'll tell you.

Solvents

All parts have to be cleaned, and most should be cleaned in solvent. There are several good solvents on the market. Bike shops have them, as do automotive and hardware stores. One good one is kerosene, available at some service stations. *Don't use gasoline!* It cleans, but it also has a very touchy flash point. Acetone is very volatile too, but is fairly safe if used in small doses on an absorbent rag.

To use solvents, you'll need a container to use as a soaker tray. That's no problem: a coffee can, a plastic bleach bottle with the top cut out; anything that will be big enough to hold the parts, but not so big it requires lots of solvent. Also, have a small soaker tray—say a mayonnaise jar lid—for loose ball bearings. Keeping them separate will aid in hanging onto all of them.

_____ **Where do you get parts?**

After you have figured out what's wrong and how to fix it, you may need to buy parts. Where do you go? Usually, the bike shop is your best bet. If you bought your bike through a bicycle dealer, he will also stock parts for your bike. A good bike dealer who is in the repair business will also stock parts for all sorts of bikes other than the ones he sells.

Most towns will have more than one repair shop. It won't take you very long to find out which dealer really cares about you and your bike. He may be young or old, he may have a modern or an ancient-looking shop. He may or may not be an authorized dealer for one of the popular makes of bikes. He'll be the kind of guy who will take a few minutes to talk about your problems. He'll not mind looking for a small washer that may only cost a few pennies. If you need something that he doesn't have in stock, he will know where to order it and won't mind doing so. He will also employ only the kind of help that will be like he is with regard to your bike. Once you have found this guy, treat him right. Don't ask tough-to-explain questions when he's loaded with customers. When you decide not to do-it-yourself, give him the repair job. Buy all your parts, accessories, and future bikes from him. Tout him to your cycling friends. In short, show him you appreciate his interest in your bike. A good cycle-analyst is hard to find.

There are several mail-order parts houses. If you live in a small town, or if you can't find that right dealer or repair shop, they will stock or get anything you need. They won't save you any money; in most cases, you even have to pay for their catalog. By the time you place an order, the price list they sent you has usually been superseded, so the money you sent isn't quite enough. It takes time to process your order and get the post office to deliver it. If you're like me, you don't figure out what all you'll need until you have the bike apart, and you want to get the part *now*. So the local dealer has an advantage there. Also, most mail-order houses have a minimum of two or three dollars, and if you need a few nuts and wash-

29

ers, you have to end up buying things you don't need to get them to ship what you want.

The mail-order parts companies I know of are

> Big Wheel, Ltd.
> 340 Holly St.
> Denver, Colo. 80220
>
> Cyclo-Pedia
> 311 N. Mitchell
> Cadillac, Mich. 49601
>
> Wheel Goods Corp.
> 2737 Hennepin Ave.
> Minneapolis, Minn. 55408

All three have catalogs—for a price.

Sometimes you won't be able to buy the one tiny part you need. Your bike man doesn't have it, and the manufacturer is one of the few that just won't mess with a one-part order. Before you buy an entire assembly, see if there might be an almost identical part that will do the job. That's where a good cycle-analyst really pays off. He'll know what will interchange and what won't.

> Remember this RULE OF THUMB: *Don't dismantle your machine on the days when the repair shop where you get parts is closed.*

Maintenance Racks

To work on the gears, the rear wheel, or the chain, you almost have to have the rear wheel off the ground. The old standby is to turn the machine upside down, resting it on the seat and handlebars. However, if your handlebars are any of several types, or if your cables or levers stick up above the bars, this may not be a very easy thing to do. In fact, it's a bad idea. That's why we'd like to recommend that you rig up a bike rack.

If your bike is to be flipped over for work, place a newspaper under the seat. Place 2" × 4" blocks under the handlebars to keep cables or levers from touching the ground. One friend rigged up an additional helper in the form of a holder to prevent the bike from falling over while working on it. He employed guy wires attached to eye screws in a wooden frame in which the seat and handlebars rested. However, if you are going to go to that much trouble, you could just as easily build one of the maintenance racks.

Whatever kind of rack you rig, make it so the bike will be high enough for you to work on it without having to bend over in a back-breaking position. Most cyclers who do all their own maintenance and repairs fix a rack so they can sit on a stool while fiddling with the machine. Planning on this from the

FIGURE 18

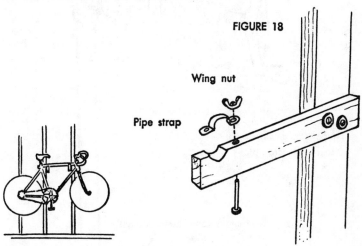

Wing nut

Pipe strap

1″ × 4″ bolted to two studs on garage wall. Add a brace if needed—or if studs aren't exposed, a freestanding pair of 2″ × 4″s on a base could be rigged.

start will help. Also, try to rig the rack so you can move all around the bike. This is not always possible, but is certainly always desirable. The two rack designs illustrated in Figures 18 and 19 require no explanation and are fairly easy to construct. If you come up with a clever rack design of your own, shoot it along to me and I'll find a way to pass it on to fellow bikers—either in my syndicated column or through some magazine articles I've been asked to write.

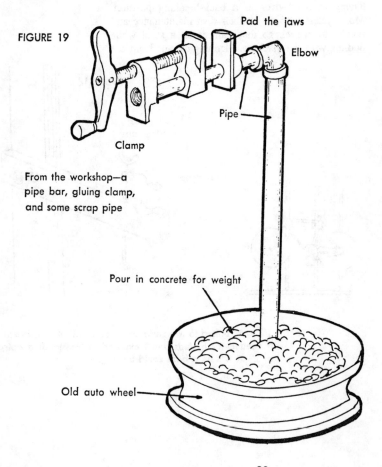

FIGURE 19

Pad the jaws

Elbow

Pipe

Clamp

From the workshop—a
pipe bar, gluing clamp,
and some scrap pipe

Pour in concrete for weight

Old auto wheel

32

7

General Rules
of Thumb

You'll find other rules and other thumbs scattered throughout the book. The ones below apply to more than just one section.

1. Unless otherwise stated, to tighten a bolt or screw, turn *clockwise;* and to loosen, *counterclockwise*. (Figure 20.) Or maybe you'd rather remember the old Super Handyman rule, "Right is tight, left is loose." Or the other one, "Clockwise is lockwise."

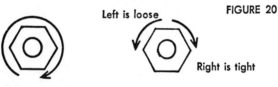

FIGURE 20

Left is loose

Right is tight

Clockwise is lockwise

2. The "Right side" of the bike refers to the right side of the bicycle if you were riding it.

3. Don't overtighten any threaded parts.

4. Always try to make an adjustment before you dismantle.

5. Maintenance is better than repair—and a heck of a lot easier.

6. Use proper tools. A slightly too large wrench can chew up a nut or bolt. A pair of pliers instead of a wrench can chew up and spit out a nut or bolt.

7. Lubrication is a must. The whole world loves a luber, and so will your bike.

8. If you have to dismantle part of your bike, thus exposing other parts, check, clean, and lube the newly exposed other parts. (This can lead to a complete overhaul, but it's worth it.)

9. Keep track of the parts and their sequence. It's extremely important to get everything back on the way it came off. Sometimes your parts may differ from my drawing, so let your bike—not the illustration—be your final authority.

10. When clamping a part in a vise or pliers, pad it so it won't get scratched. Sometimes masking tape around the part will be enough protection. Other times you may need blocks of wood or foam rubber between part and clamp.

11. Unless otherwise stated, when you finish cleaning parts, always give them a coat of light oil—machine oil will do. When there's a need for heavier oil or no oil at all, I'll tell you.

8

Seats

Adjusting the seat is a simple but very important task. The seat can be adjusted for height and angle.

To adjust the height:

8A-1. Loosen the nut at the top of the seat tube. See Figure 21 You don't have to remove it, just loosen it.

FIGURE 21

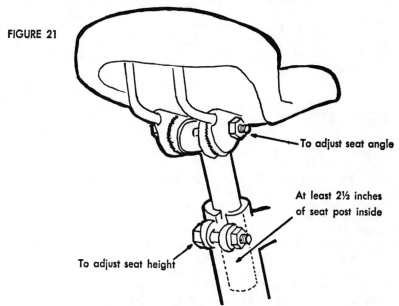

To adjust seat angle

At least 2½ inches
of seat post inside

To adjust seat height

8A-2. Pull the seat up or push down to raise or lower. You may have to twist it from side to side as you push or pull.

8A-3. When the right height is reached, retighten. See Chapter 3 for proper height. Be sure it's tight!

RULE OF THUMB: *Always have at least 2½ inches of seat post down inside the seat tube. Otherwise, the seat can come loose unexpectedly and painfully. If there's any doubt, pull the post all the way out. If the rider is growing, it's even a good idea to etch a line at the 2½-inch mark.*

To adjust the angle:

8B-1. Loosen the nut or nuts at the clamp at the top of the seat post. See Figure 21.

8B-2. Grab the front and back of the saddle and tilt it up or back as needed.

8B-3. Retighten the nut and take a ride around the block. Be sure it's tight!

If you have to replace the seat post, get one the same diameter as the old one. A too-big post could perhaps be forced in, but it might stretch the tube and create a weak spot.

The tired seat, or the saga of the sagging saddle

Seats come in many different varieties—yes, even bicycle seats. Usually, the only thing that goes wrong with the sitting part of the saddle is that the leather or plastic wears through. In most cases, you don't need to buy an entire seat. Unless the cover is fastened on with rivets or brads, it will be easy to slip it off and replace. Take the old cover with you to get the right size. Some seats require the removal of the sissy bars to remove the cover. These, too, may be riveted on, and it may not be worth the trouble.

About the only other seat tragedy is that it may start sagging. Whatever the type seat you have, you should be able to look at it and see if there isn't something you can do to firm it up. The best way to see what you're doing is to remove the seat from the frame. See Procedure 8B for the way to go. Then if the cover is removable, slip it off. Under here there will probably be a molded plastic or metal seat. If it's metal, it could be bent, or if it's plastic, it could be cracked. Only you will be able to determine if it's worth trying to fix. If this part is shot, only on a very few can replacements be made, and finding the replacement is even rarer.

Next, check the springs. Most saddles have some sort. If there are a series of long skinny springs that run more or less parallel to the seat, check them over. There may be one that has lost its pizazz. One may have come unhooked, or there may be one missing. Get a new one and hook it into the holes, and you're ready to go. If the springs are coils of wire that bounce you up and down, check to see if they are even. Usually a little rebending will set them straight. If they can't be repaired, you may have a problem getting a new set.

Some seats can be tightened by adjusting the metal frame over which the cover is stretched. If that's the kind you have, you'll find a nut under the front of the seat. By tightening this, the frame is pushed out longer and thus stretches the seat cover out tight.

9

Handlebars

_____ **Adjusting Handlebars**

Handlebar height and angle is important to your comfort and safety. The handlebar and the accessories that are on it should be positioned so you can stop, ring, honk, toot, or whatever without lessening your control.

To raise or lower handlebars:

9A-1. Loosen the expander bolt in the top of the stem (Figure 22).

9A-2. When the bolt has risen about ¼ inch, tap it so the wedge nut moves down to relieve the pressure holding it.

9A-3. Now raise or lower the handlebar by twisting it from side to side while you push or pull.

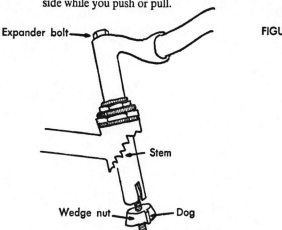

Expander bolt

FIGURE 22

Stem

Wedge nut — Dog

38

9A-4. Straighten the handlebar in relation to the wheel.

9A-5. Tighten the expander bolt.

RULE OF THUMB: *At least 2½ inches of stem are down in the headset. If there's any doubt, remove and mark the 2½-inch spot.*

To adjust the angle or tilt to the bars:

9B-1. Loosen the clamp bolt. (Some are on top as opposed to the one in Figure 23.)

9B-2. Grab bars and rotate within the clamp to suit your needs.

9B-3. Retighten and make sure it's tight.

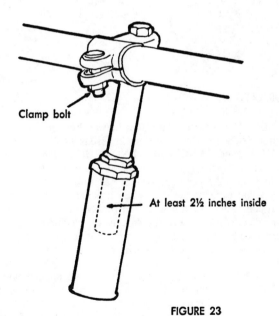

Clamp bolt

At least 2½ inches inside

FIGURE 23

39

_____ **Taping Your Handlebars**

Most of the sporty lightweight jobs with drop bars, maes, or touring bend bars are wrapped with tape. The tapes come in great colors that can either match the paint on your bike or introduce another color (maybe to match your eyes). The tape also provides a more comfortable grip. Older bikes with bad chrome on the handlebars can be made to look new by covering up the pitted places with tape.

In choosing the tape, there are two kinds—adhesive and nonadhesive. Personally, I like the nonadhesive, but I certainly want you to make up your

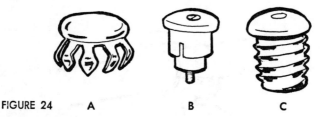

FIGURE 24   A   B   C

own mind. If you agree on the nonadhesive, here are the simple steps to follow. All you will need is TAPE, SOLVENT, and HANDLEBAR END PLUGS. Plug A, the most popular type, is chrome and runs about fifty to sixty cents per pair. Plug B has a screw in the end that expands the plug when it is set in the bar. It comes in colored plastics and rubber. Plug C, also made of plastic in several colors, is threaded and is turned in place. There are many variations, but these are the basic types. Now you're ready to begin.

9C-1.   If your bike already has old tape, remove the end plugs, pull the end of the old tape out of the handlebar, and unwrap it.

9C-2.   Now take the solvent and clean and dry the bar. (A *Side Step:* While the bar is unwrapped, it's a good time to move the brake lever if it's not just where you want it. See Chapter 12 for this.)

9C-3. Start wrapping about 2 inches from the center of the handle-bar. Use a piece of electrician's tape on the very end to hold

FIGURE 25

it in place if you wish. However, this isn't really necessary. Make a double layer at the beginning. Be sure to pull the tape tightly as you wrap it around.

9C-4. Now continue wrapping toward the end. Make sure that each wrap overlaps the previous round by about ¼ inch.

9C-5. When you get to the brake lever, bring the tape tight around the base, forming a *V* around the lever housing. Remember to keep it tight all along.

FIGURE 26

9C-6. Now continue the overlapping wrap all the way to the end.

9C-7. When you reach the end, keep wrapping right on off, and then clip the tape, leaving about 3 inches left over.

9C-8. Holding it tight around the bar, poke the excess into the end of the bar and insert the plug.

FIGURE 27

If you didn't do it right, unwrap the whole deal and try again. *You can do it!*

If you decided on the adhesive-backed handlebar tape, follow the same procedures as in nonadhesive, using steps 9C-1 and 9C-2.

> **9C-3a.** With the clean dry bar, start at the *end* of the bar and work back toward the center. Overlap as you go and do the same thing around the brake lever as in step C-5 above.
>
> **9C-4a.** When you get about 2 inches from the center, make a double wrap and cut the tape.

Tape is fairly inexpensive, and you've mastered the art of wrapping. Instead of a paint job on the old frame, wrap it in the color of tape that suits your fancy. It will look great and can be done without dismantling the bike as is necessary for a painting.

One of the readers of my column suggested that handlebars with end plugs make a nice place to hide mad money, an address card to help prove it's yours if it is stolen—or whatever you've got to hide.

Coming to grips with your grips

So we didn't talk you into wrapping your handlebars! You still dig your old handlegrips. OK, just make sure they are tight. A loose grip can cause an accident.

> **9D-1.** Take the loose job off.
>
> **9D-2.** Clean the bar with solvent.
>
> **9D-3.** Smear cement all around the bar where the grip will go. Use any kind of adhesive that claims to stick metal to rubber. Also, put adhesive inside the grip. A length of dowel will distribute the goo all around.
>
> **9D-4.** Install the grip, twisting it as you push it in place.
>
> **9D-5.** When it's all the way in, make sure the finger ridges end up underneath where your fingers will be when you grab hold.
>
> **9D-6.** Before the adhesive dries, take a rag and remove any excess that came out. Don't ride until the adhesive is set firmly.

While you have the glue out, glue a rubber tip on

the end of your kickstand. Most stands come with a tip that lasts about fourteen minutes because it's not glued on.

_____ **Bent Bars**

Handlebars rarely stand up under the strain of a car backing over them. If you're careful and don't leave your bike behind cars, there are other ways to bend them. If the metal isn't cracked, and if the bend isn't bad, it's worth a try at straightening. You'll have to remove the bar.

9E-1. Take the grip or tape wrapping from one side.
9E-2. Remove all accessories attached to the bar.
9E-3. Loosen the clamp bolt (also called binder bolt).
9E-4. Twist the bar in the clamp while pulling on the side that still has the grip.

With the bar out, you can try to bend it back in shape. How to do this will depend on how it's bent. Avoid the temptation to get out the mallet until the more gradual methods have failed. If it needs to be pulled out, clamp one end in a vise (padded, of course), hook it over something, or get a friend to hold the other end. Pull and see if you can't straighten it by hand. If that won't work, try the tourniquet method described in Chapter 11.

If it needs to be pushed in, brace it against something and push. The tourniquet method may work here too.

Even if you straighten it, the bending may have weakened the metal. Watch it to see if any splits or cracks appear, and replace it at the first sign.

If you can't straighten it, a new one won't break the bank. Be sure to get one of the same diameter so it'll fit the clamp.

10

Tires, Wheels, and Spokes

Tires

Properly operated, the only contact your bike ever has with the road is through its tires. From that statement, a third grader would know that this must be an important part of any bicycle. But most cyclers don't pay any attention to the tires until one goes completely flat. Bike tires should last for thousands of miles—with proper care. We've spoken earlier about the importance of proper tire pressure. Improper tire pressure is the single most destructive force on bike tires. Don't judge by looks alone. Use a pressure gauge and keep the right amount of air in your tires.

Many other things can affect the life of your tires: wheel alignment, brake adjustment, rim damage. All are covered in the other sections that deal with these parts.

So . . . what if the tire doesn't hold air?

First, you have to know what type of tires you have. Although there are dozens of different treads, body construction materials, and even colors to match your frame, there are still just two basic types of bike tires in common usage—the clincher and the tubular. The clincher type has a separate tube, and the tubular type doesn't. (Confusing terminology, isn't it?) The clincher type is basically like the old style auto tires—an open casing that is held against the rim when there is air pressure in the tube to push against

FIGURE 28

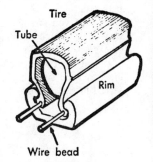

Clincher tire

44

it. The tubulars, or sew-ups, have a tube that is completely encased in the tire. The tire is held to the rim by means of special cement that is applied to both the tire and the rim—and often to your hands and clothes.

Whatever type you have, you must determine what is causing the air to leak out before you start to fix it. Unless you see a railroad spike sticking into the tire or something equally obvious, check to see if the valve is the culprit. This involves the Saliva Test. With air in the tire and with the valve cap removed, drool on your finger and cover the valve with spit. If it bubbles, see if the valve stem needs tightening. There are three different types of valves, and there is a sketch of each basic type in Figure 30. If you have

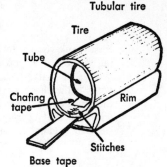

Tubular tire

FIGURE 29

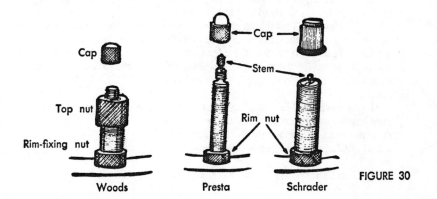

FIGURE 30

Woods   Presta   Schrader

the Woods or the Presta type, you have already discovered that it presents problems. Regular pumps won't screw on the valve, and you have to have a special tire gauge. If you haven't already discovered it, there is an adapter pump connector that converts an import valve so that an American hand pump fits on it. The most common type valve is the one on the end known as the Schrader. It's found on clincher tires, and the others are found on tubulars.

If tightening or replacing the valve core doesn't work—or if the valve passed the saliva test to begin with—you'll need to remove the tire to find the leak.

FIGURE 31

First check visually for anything that might be sticking in the tire. If you spot something, circle it with a piece of chalk. Also, make a mark on the rim if yours is the clincher type. This will help you to find the punctured place in the tube after the wheel, tire, and tube are separated. Let's first go through the steps in patching a clincher-type flat.

10A-1. If you can spot the culprit—let's say it's a nail—you can probably repair the tube without removing the wheel. If there is still air in the tire, remove the valve stem and let the air out.

10A-2. Next, go all around the tire and push it inward at the rim to unstick tire and rim.

10A-3. With the tire unstuck all around, you should be able to grip the tread and roll it away from you.

10A-4. This should reveal enough edge of the tire so you can reach in with a finger and slip the edge out over the rim.

10A-5. Now pull the edge out all the way around or at least far enough to pull out the portion of tube that has the hole.

If you have trouble removing the tire with your bare hands, resist the temptation to use a screwdriver as a pry bar. Remember those tire tools we talked about in Chapter 6? Here's how to use 'em.

RULE of THUMB: *Don't . . . unless you have to!*

Really give it the old college try with your bare hands, but if it's too tight, then you'll have to use the irons. Just be supercareful not to pinch the tube or split the bead. Here's how:

10B-1. Slip the rounded plain end of the tool against the deflated tire and ease it under the bead on that side. Start at a spoke.

10B-2. With the iron (they're also called tire levers) under the bead, bring the other end back and all the way around until it's against the spoke.

10B-3. If it's still under the bead, hook the slot over the spoke as shown in Figure 32.

10B-4. Slip a second iron in next to the first . . . carefully . . . and lift out more bead.

10B-5. Once the section of pried-out tire isn't trying to hop back in, you've pried enough. Remove the tools and take it off the rest of the way by hand as directed in 10A-2.

FIGURE 32

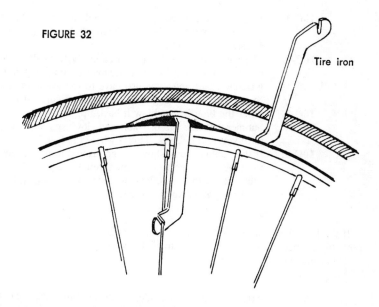

Tire iron

If you pinched the tube, patch it along with the original flaw and be more careful next time!

For the actual patching job, get a patch kit. There are cold patch and hot patch types. The cold patch is more compact. It will have everything you need, including patches, cement, a graterlike top for roughing up the surface of the tube, and THE INSTRUCTIONS. Each kit will give you specific instructions for its use.

47

RULE OF THUMB: *Clean the tube well where the patch will go—rubbing alcohol on a rag will do the job. Rough it up well. Cut a patch big enough, and then be sure you smear on enough cement to cover an area bigger than the patch. Don't touch the sticky side of the patch after you've peeled off the backing.*

10C-1. If there is a leak, but you didn't find the cause, then you will have to remove the wheel and take the tube completely out of the tire.

10C-2. The valve should be removed carefully from the hole in the rim. You may have to remove a rim-fixing nut. It unscrews, and you may also have to remove a valve cap to get the valve through the hole. (See Figure 30.)

10C-3. After the tube is out, blow it back up.

10C-4. Submerge it in a tub of water and slowly go all around it until you find bubbles. This is where the leak is.

10C-5. If the bubbles don't show up, go around again, squeezing the tube as you go to force air through the leak. Grip the tube with both hands, leaving about 3 inches of tube between as you move all around it.

If the leak shows up around the valve stem, you'll probably do better to invest in a new tube. It won't cost that much.

10C-6. After your patch is made, inflate the tube again and test it before you put it back in. It will probably be OK, but it's a lot easier to find out now than to have to take the entire thing apart again. Also check for additional leaks. A nail or a long thorn could have gone through the tube twice.

10C-7. Also, check the inside of the tire for any possible sharp points that may have caused the leak. Slip your hand in an old nylon stocking and feel around inside. The nylon snags on everything.

10C-8. It's a good idea to lightly sprinkle the inside casing with talcum powder. This keeps the tire and the tube from sticking together. (If you have to remove the whole she-bang, it's a good opportunity to check the rim over too.)

10C-9. If the rim has a rubber rim strip, line up the hole in it with the valve stem hole in the rim.

10C-10. Take the empty tire casing and slip one edge on the rim all the way around. If you have trouble getting the last few inches of bead to slip over the rim, don't give up—and don't reach for that pry bar. Keep working with your bare hands, and eventually it will go on.

10C-11. You are now ready to stuff the tube back into the tire. Start by inserting the valve stem into its hole. Be sure it is straight up and down. If it's at an angle now, it could rip the stem out of its socket when air pressure is added.

10C-12. Work the tube in place, going in both directions from the stem.

10C-13. When the tube is back in all around, it's a good idea to slightly inflate it (5 lbs.) to remove any kinks or wrinkles. You'll be able to see if it's straight all the way around.

10C-14. Now you are ready for the chore of getting the other bead back in place inside the rim. Everything will go smoothly as long as you make sure you don't pinch the tube between the rim and the bead—that is, until you get to the last 4 to 5 inches. Then you will find the bead doesn't want to go over the rim. *Don't reach for the pry bar*—remember the old adage, "All things come to him who waits . . . and strains like crazy." Keep pushing with both thumbs in one spot on the bead until it slips over. (It will.)

10C-15. Now move over to the next spot. Eventually, your patience and pulled thumb muscles will be rewarded. Get the kids out of the way during this step, as they often don't understand the four-letter bike repair terms that sometimes help at such times.

10C-16. Inflate it again slightly (10 lbs. this time). Check to be sure the bead is properly seated all around the rim on both sides. Also, at this time, check the valve stem again to be sure it's still sticking straight up. If not, completely deflate the tire, and holding the spokes, slide the tire in the direction that will move the tube to straighten the valve.

10C-17. If the stem is straight, bounce the tire lightly, turning it around as you go. This takes care of any kinks or wrinkles that developed while you got the tire back on.

10C-18. Deflate again. This makes sure the tube lets go if it's being pinched in the casing.

10C-19. Now you are ready to put the wheel back on. See Procedure 10E.

The tubular, or sew-up, tire is a different colored horse. You also need a repair kit—this one especially for tubular tires. It will probably contain patches, fine sandpaper, needle, thread, thimble, patch cement, rim cement, and THE INSTRUCTIONS . . . and a prayer.

10D-1. To patch a tubular, the tire must be taken off the wheel, which is one disadvantage already.

10D-2. You're now ready to remove the tire from the rim. This is where you've a big advantage. It's easy. Take off the cap and lock nut from the valve stem and deflate the tire —if it's not already flat. Roll the tire off the rim 180° from the valve. It's a snap. When it's rolled off all the way around, push the valve stem out, and it's off!

10D-3. When dunking the tire to try to locate the leak, you'll find that bubbles will come out around the valve. This may or may not be your trouble. It may mean that part of the air that is escaping is trapped inside the casing until it gets to the valve which offers an easier way out than through the casing, chafing tape, base tape, and stitching. If you think I just made up all those things, look back at Figure 29 to see just how a tubular tire is made up. After the correct leaking area is located, keep going around the tire under the water to be sure that's the only place.

10D-4. Mark the place or places with chalk.

10D-5. You are ready to find the tube inside. First, you must lift the base tape for about 6 inches along the place where you think the puncture is. You will now see the stitching that holds the casing together.

10D-6. Mark a line alongside each stitch. A fine-line felt marker or a ball-point will do.

10D-7. Now you are ready to cut the stitching. Cut only one place and then pick the stitches out with a hook of some sort.

FIGURE 33

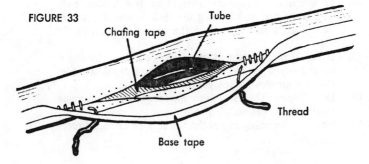

Tube

Chafing tape

Thread

Base tape

10D-8. Now you can see the chafing tape. Lift this up, and *voilà* the tube is underneath.

10D-9. Pull the tube out far enough, and if the hole isn't apparent, inflate and dunk to find exactly where it is. Dry the water off completely. Chalk to mark patch area. The patches work like the cold patch for the clincher-type tube.

The same general rules apply: Clean, rough up, cement, and apply the patch. Follow the instructions.

10D-10. Sprinkle the talc around after you have finished the patching and the cement is dry. Make sure you do a good job. The talc will keep any excess cement from sticking to the tape or the casing.

10D-11. Put the tube back in and replace the chafing tape. Line up the thread holes by looking at the marks.

10D-12. You are now ready to become a seamstress. Thread the needle with the loose end of the thread, and using the existing holes, carefully restitch the tire. When you have as much of the old thread back in, rethread your needle and knot the end. Use only enough new thread to overlap the ends of the old thread.

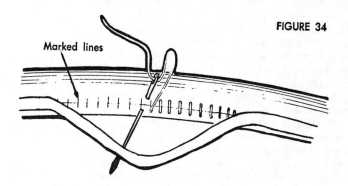

FIGURE 34

Marked lines

10D-13. When you have closed the casing and tied off the thread, smear the underside of the base tape with tire cement, and also coat the area you have stitched. Most kits will direct you to wait until the cement becomes tacky before pressing the base tape back smoothly in place.

10D-14. You are ready to put the tire back on the rim. Here is where it's easy compared with the clincher type. Your four-letter bike terms won't be needed. Remove all the old rim cement with solvent or rubbing alcohol. Wipe dry.

10D-15. Apply a new layer of cement all around the rim. Remember this is *rim cement,* not tire cement. Let this dry until tacky.

10D-16. With the tire completely deflated, start by reinserting the valve. Working from the valve and going both directions, start pushing the tire back in place over the rim. When you have worked all the way around, the last few inches will go on easily with little extra thumb pressure.

10D-17. Partially inflate the tire (15 lbs.). Check to see that the treads are straight all the way around and are centered on the rim. If not, deflate and move the tire into position with your hands.

10D-18. Now inflate to the proper pressure and install the valve lock nut and the valve cap.

10D-19. Reinstall the wheel as per Procedures 10E (front) and 10G (rear).

You think you're ready to ride? Not yet. The cement needs to be held against the rim by the air pressure overnight so it will adhere properly before riding.

Taking care of your tires will pay off with longer life. Well-cared-for tires will last for years and years until the rubber starts to deteriorate. If the tread starts to go, and you don't have the traction you'd like, you may want to try a product called Black Strap. It's actually a sole saver for shoes, but it also can add traction to your bike tires. So many people have used it for this that the manufacturer now includes separate instructions for tire recapping.

Most of us don't have flats enough to need more than a hand pump. This is hard work, but when all you're doing is adding a few pounds of pressure periodically to keep it up to snuff, this is an inexpensive way to go. Pumping up a completely flat tire to its riding pressure gets pretty tedious, so you may wish to pump it up part way, and then toss it into the back of the station wagon for a trip to the service station for the rest of the pressure.

Pressure Chart for Tires

RULE OF THUMB: *Keep tires inflated hard.*

Tire Size	Weight of Cycler			
	125 lbs. & under	150	175	200
27" x 1¼"	75	80	80	85
1¼" (not 27"s)	45	55	60	65
1⅜"	45	50	55	60
1½"	40	45	50	55
1¾"	35	40	45	50
Racing				
27" tubular				
front	70	75	80	85
rear	75	80	85	90
Touring				
27" tubular				
front	75	80	85	90
	85	90	95	100

OTHER RULES OF THUMB: *Protect tires and tubes from contact with oil. Make sure no oil sneaks down the spokes from the hub. Keep tires and tubes away from solvents. After a road trip, wipe tires to remove any oil you may have picked up.*

Wheel Removal

This is a very easy task. In fact, I've known wheels to remove themselves—which is a good reason to know how they come off and go back on.

First, let's take off the front wheel. Before you start, if you have caliper brakes, be sure the pads are far enough apart to remove the wheel. Unless you have a quick-release brake lever, you may have to loosen the cable anchor nut to slacken the cable.

RULE OF THUMB: *Don't pull the cable end out—it won't want to go back in.*

10E-1.	Rack your bike—or somehow get the front wheel off the ground.
10E-2.	Remove axle nuts—or if you have quick-release hubs, turn the lever so it points out.
10E-3.	If you have mudguards (fenders) with braces that fit over the axle, they'll need to be spread.
10E-4.	Wheel should be eased down and forward to get it out of the fork.

To put the front wheel back on just follow these steps in reverse order.

Be sure to get the axle up against the drop out. Also, make sure the wheel is centered in the fork.

The rear wheel is something else. There are three basic types: (1) 1-speeds with coaster brakes, (2) multispeed hubs, and (3) derailleurs with their free-wheel clusters.

10F-1.	Get your wheel off the ground.
10F-2.	If you have gears, a multispeed hub is shifted into high gear. A derailleur-geared bike should be shifted so the chain is on the smallest rear sprocket of the cluster.
10F-3.	If you have a coaster brake, undo the small nut and bolt holding the clip that holds the brake arm to the left chain stay.
10F-4.	If you have caliper brakes, be sure the brake shoes are far enough apart to remove the wheel. If you have a quick-release lever on your brake, this will allow you to spread the shoes with a flip of the wrist. Otherwise, you'll probably have to loosen the cable anchor. The same rule of thumb applies: Don't let the cable slip all the way out!
10F-5.	Getting back to multispeed hubs, you'll want to loosen the cable lock nut and twist the adjusting screw off to unhook the cable.

54

10F-6. Undo the axle nuts on either side of the bike, or, if you have a quick-release hub, turn the lever so it points straight out.

10F-7. On non-derailleur bikes, just slip the wheel out of the drop outs and lift the chain from around the rear sprocket.

10F-8. Derailleur bikes come off just as easily, but you'll need to pull the changer out of the way as you slip the wheel out of the drop outs. Once out, you can lift the chain from around the small rear sprocket.

If you have washers on either side of the frame, be sure to note exactly where they are so you get the wheel back on the way it should be.

Getting the back wheel back on is no problem—it's the reverse order of what we just went through. Only there is more to mess with. I've noted a few things that either make the job easier or are worth a reminder.

10G-1. Unscrew the axle nuts so they're almost to the end of the axle.

10G-2. Don't forget to place the chain over the sprocket before you slip the axle back into the drop outs—smallest sprocket if you have a cluster!

10G-3. Non-derailleur bikes require nothing but slipping the axle into the drop outs, sliding them back until the chain has about ½ inch of play at the center point between the front and the rear sprockets. When it gets there, turn the axle nuts down tight.

10G-4. Bikes with derailleur-equipped gears are a little different. Get the wheel in place in the drop outs and slip the chain over the small sprocket. Now push the axle back so the right end of the axle is all the way back in its slit. Hold it there and move the left end until the wheel is exactly centered between the two chain stays. When it's there, tighten both axle nuts.

10G-5. If you have quick-release hubs, hold the nut on the right end and rotate the unit two turns counterclockwise. Fit the right end of the axle all the way back in the slot. Line up the wheel so it's exactly centered in the two chain stays. When it's there, rotate the lever end clockwise until it's finger tight. Then snap the lever to lock it.

10G-6. Check after locking the wheel back on to make sure it's still centered.

10G-7. Put it all back together. Connect the cable on multispeeds, and adjust. Secure the brake arm on coaster brakes, and reconnect the cable on caliper brakes. Adjust, if you had to undo.

10G-8. Road test.

_____ **Spokes**

If you have established that there is a bum spoke that cannot be straightened, you will want to replace it. This is no big chore, and in many cases can be done without deflating the tire. Before you make a judgment on whether to deflate the tire and remove the wheel, be sure to check to see that the nipple is still in good condition. The next thing to ascertain is whether or not you can get to the hole in the hub where the spoke is to be replaced. This is not going to be any big chore on the front wheel, but many times you run into a sprocket or freewheel assembly on the rear wheel that has to be moved out of the way. Some rear sprockets have slots so that by adjusting the sprocket you can thread a spoke through and get it in place without removing the sprocket. If you happen to run across a front wheel that has to be removed, go back to Procedure 10E. For a back wheel, check 10F. The simple steps needed in the removal of a tire are in 10A. If you lucked out and have to remove the wheel and the tire, you may also find that you have to remove a rubber band seal that is around the rim. Now you can get at the nipple as shown in the diagram in Figure 35. This nipple may not look exactly like the ones on your bike, but they are all fairly similar.

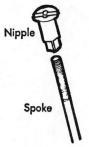

Nipple

Spoke

FIGURE 35

10H-1. Here we go again. You've been working for fifteen minutes and have just now come to the first step. Whether the tire is off or on, the first thing to do is take a spoke wrench (you could use pliers, but you'd probably chew up the nipple, and besides, the spoke wrench (Figure 36) will probably cost you only twenty-five to fifty cents). Turn it counterclockwise to loosen the spoke from the

FIGURE 36

nipple. If the spoke is frozen in the nipple, try a drop of penetrating oil and a five-minute coffee break.

10H-2. With the spoke out of the nipple, slip the old spoke through the hole in the hub, and it's out of the way.

10H-3. You've got to get a new spoke. The old one is OK to take to the shop if it hasn't been bent too badly out of shape, or if it hasn't broken. If you feel that it is not a good enough sample to take, then I would suggest that you take a good spoke *from the same side* of the wheel to get your replacement in exactly the same length, diameter, and thread type. If you can get everything else right, and it's just a tiny bit too long, the spoke can be cut off, but make very sure that you don't botch up the threads in doing so.

10H-4. If you are replacing the nipple, you have to be sure that you get the exact same kind of nipple.

10H-5. Next, all you have to do is stick the threaded end of the spoke through the hole in the hub and pull it up so the head is against the hole. One thing you want to be sure to note is that the heads alternate, with every other one being inside the hub or outside.

If you were able to attempt the spoke replacement without taking the tire off, you'll have to bend the spoke a little bit so that you can guide the threads into the nipple. Make sure that your replacement spoke follows the same pattern as all the other spokes in the wheel: spokes with the head on the inside cross over on the outside of the spokes with the head on the outside. This is particularly important to watch when you're going to have to replace

57

more than one spoke. Once the spoke is poked into the nipple, you can start turning with your fingers at first. And then you can get it reasonably well screwed in with the spoke wrench.

If you were lucky enough to have to remove the wheel and tire, the slotted-type nipples can be engaged and turned down tight with a screwdriver more easily than by using the spoke wrench.

Getting spokes in proper adjustment is the key to a wheel that turns straight and true. If there is some doubt about your wheel being true, we'll take care of that in the very next section. However, if you have added only one or two spokes, and your wheel was in great shape before (great shape for a wheel is totally round), then you'll want to adjust only the new spokes. A popular method is the musical method —you pluck the older spokes with your finger like a guitar string. Keeping that sound in mind, you then tighten the new spoke so that it's in tune with the old spoke. This may sound a little bit ridiculous, but it really does work.

One other way that works fairly well is to check the ends of the old spokes to see just how much thread is showing from under the nipple. By adjusting the new spokes so that the same number of threads are sticking out from the nipple, you'll end up with the new spokes adjusted. If you can't get the new spokes adjusted this way, you may have to go through the procedure of truing your wheel.

Truing a Rim

The wheels of your bicycle were meant to be completely, truly round. While the drawing in Figure 37 is an exaggeration, when you get a wheel that is out of round, even slightly, it can make riding your bicycle feel as if you've got square wheels. Also, assuming that the hub is properly adjusted and there's no side play, there should be absolutely no wobble in the plane in which the wheel turns. An out-of-round and wobbly wheel can have a bad effect on many other parts of your machine.

Loosen spokes here

Tighten spokes here

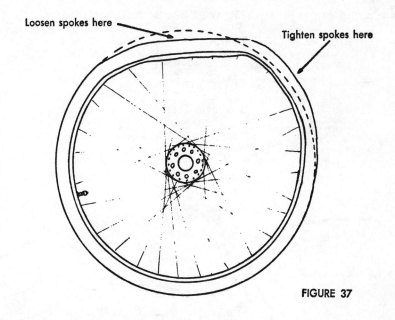

FIGURE 37

To true your wheel properly, you're going to have to remove the wheel and remove the tire. If you have a rubber band seal around the rim, this will have to be removed too. It would be great if you had a device called a truing jig—but as you probably don't, the best thing you can do is put it back in the drop out with nothing else attached so that the rim can rotate freely. You have to be able to see what you're doing, and it therefore has to be either in the maintenance rack or turned upside down so that the fenders (mudguards) don't get in your line of vision.

First, we shall talk about the out-of-round wheel. Since it started off as a perfect circle, a wheel that is out of round has to have one place where it's pulled in and another place where it's pushed out. If it were like the one in the drawing, you would be able to pick out the bad spots with no trouble. (However, if it were like the one in the drawing, you'd probably do better just to buy a new wheel.) Usually, you can't see the places where it's pulled in and

59

pushed out, so the first thing you'll have to do is find out where the deviations are. To do this, I use the blue-chalk method. This involves holding a piece of blue chalk right next to the inside surface of the rim and spinning the wheel. The point where it's pulled in will rub against the chalk, and you'll have a mark to show where it's pulled in. To find out where it's pulled out, you need to hold the blue chalk at the outside of the rim and spin it around. To do this properly, you'll have to have a much steadier hand than most of us or you'll end up mark-

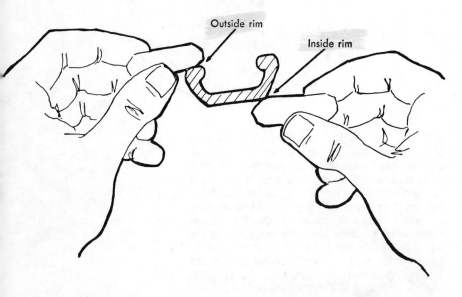

Outside rim

Inside rim

FIGURE 38

ing the wrong place or missing the bad place.

Brace the chalk and your hand against either the truing jig which you don't have or some part of your bicycle. After you have done this on one side of the rim, go around to the other side and try it there. If the marks line up, then you've found the bad places. If they don't line up, check to be sure that the wheel is straight in the jig and that it's not loose. (My biggest problem with the blue-chalk method is that I can never find my blue chalk. As a substitute, you can take a wax crayon, and it'll show up rather well.)

OK, you've now found the place where it's pulled in and the place where it's pulled out. To get it back into a perfect round shape, you're going to have to loosen spokes at the pulled-in-place and tighten them at the pushed-out place. If the pulled-in place measures 6 inches along on your rim, you have to loosen spokes all the way along. The spokes in the middle part of the marked area will have to be loosened a little more than those at the edges. For this process, your screwdriver in the slotted rim end of the nipple will work best. Rub the chalk marks off and give it the blue-chalk test again. Make the tightening and loosening cycles on a gradual basis, and keep testing until you've got it into a perfect circle. After the initial loosening and tightening, the fine tuning, so to speak, should usually be done at only a half-turn at a time.

Make sure no spoke ends come up through the nipple where they could puncture a tire. If so, they must be snipped or filed off.

Now we're ready to take a look at the side-to-side wobble. Lots of times you'll want to remedy a side-to-side wobble without going through the complete truing process, and this can often be done with the tire still in place.

If you want to check for wobble, you can rack your bike and spin the wheel with blue chalk as close as possible to the part of the rim that sticks out the farthest. If you have a bicycle with caliper brakes, you can squeeze the brakes almost to the point where they touch the rim, and by spinning the wheel and looking straight down on the tire, you'll find out if there is any wobble. If there is, you'll still have to use the blue-chalk method to mark the point where the wobble is.

In the case of a front wheel or a rear wheel with only one sprocket, the tires and rims should be centered exactly over the center of the hub. If you have a freewheel cluster, then the back wheel will be "dished." This means that the spokes on the left-hand side are a little bit longer than the spokes on

61

the right-hand side so that the wheel is actually centered between the lock nuts instead of on the hub.

Once you have located the wobble, you can correct it by loosening the spokes on the bump side and tightening the spokes on the other side by the same number of turns. In other words, if you have to move a section of the rim to the left a little bit, let's say you loosen three spokes on the right a half-turn each, you should then tighten three spokes on the left a half-turn each. This will move the rim to the left, and yet not take it out of round.

This too is a slow process of loosening and tightening and chalking.

If you've found a place that is pushed out on one side, be sure that when you get ready to chalk the other side you start at a point 180° away from the bump mark, but on the other side of the rim. Otherwise, you'll end up with chalk marks on both sides. Of course, you can end up with chalk marks on both sides anyway because there may be two places where the rim is out of line. By looking, you can usually tell from the wobble which way it's pulled out of line, and the chalk marks tell you just how far the wobble goes.

Once you've completed this job, if you had to remove the tire, wheel, and so forth, follow the simple directions in Procedure 10E (front) and 10G (rear), to get the whole thing back together again.

Now that you've got the wheel back in round and the wobble out, you'll have a lot smoother ride, you won't jar your innards so much, and your brakes will work better. Your wheels won't wear out as badly, and a lot of other bad things won't happen to your bicycle quite so quickly.

_____ **A kinky rim**

If you've tried climbing stairs or curbs with your bike, you may have put a kink in your front rim. Rims are made of fairly soft metal, and it's quite possible you may be able to save it. Subtlety is the key.

10I-1. With the tire off, fit a small strip of wood inside the rim. It must span the kink so each end is resting on unkinked rim.

10I-2. Cut a similar strip for outside.

10I-3. Using a C-clamp, start pushing the two blocks toward each other (see Figure 39). The gradual clamping pressure may

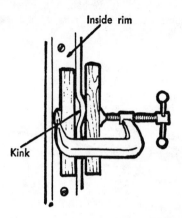

FIGURE 39

take the kink out. Watch as you turn, to be sure you're not doing any other damage to the rim.

10I-4. Don't try to beat out the kinks.

If this won't do it, take it in to your cycle-analyst and see if he thinks there's any hope.

_____ **Hubs**

You've probably already figured out that there are two hubs on most bikes—front and rear. In bicycles with derailleur gears, the two hubs are much alike. The bikes with drastically different hubs are those with coaster brakes and those with the gears in the hubs (the 3-speed jobs). The brakes and gears chapter will cover these two types, since the hubs and brakes/gears are all one big ball of wax. (No, wax is not the recommended lubricant.)

Basically speaking, the hub is the axle, its casing, two sets of bearings, cones, and the washers and locknuts that hold them.

Let's take a look at a typical front hub. To do this, you need to remove the front wheel. See Procedure 10E.

To dismantle the hub and overhaul it, the method is about the same for all except those with quick-release hubs. (See Figure 40.)

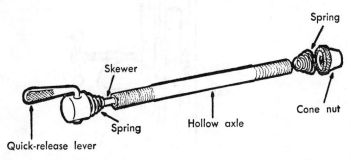

Spring

Skewer

Cone nut

Spring

Hollow axle

Quick-release lever

FIGURE 40

10J-1. The quick-release hub has a skewer that goes through the axle. It should be removed.

10J-2. Remove the adjusting nut and conical spring.

10J-3. Now the rest of the unit, including the skewer or mounting stud, will slide out of the axle. There's another conical spring that will come out with the unit. From here on in, it will be much like the other front hubs shown.

10J-4. Put the quick-release assembly loosely together and put it out of the way until you're ready to put it all together.

10J-5. Next you must remove one of the locknuts. Usually, if you'll hold one cone with a wrench and turn the locknut (or axle nut if your hub is sans locknuts) tight against it, you can turn the other locknut off.

10J-6. If you prefer to work with the wheel lying flat, place a towel or some sort of buffer under the axle—otherwise, hold the wheel upright between your legs.

10J-7. As you take the parts off the assembly, deposit them in solvent.

10J-8. When the locknut is screwed off, the washer will slide off.

10J-9. Turn the cone off.

10J-10. If there are loose bearings, there'll be a dust cap. Pry this out and prepare for your juggling act. Lift the wheel, and be sure to catch all the steel balls—count them and drop them in the solvent.

10J-11. If there are caged bearings, they slip right out.

10J-12. By pulling the other end of the axle, it will slip right out. (You didn't forget the loose bearings on the other end, did you?)

10J-13. Before you remove the other cone from the axle, measure its distance from the end of the axle. This'll help when you get ready to get it all together again.

10J-14. Drag out an old toothbrush and clean all the parts and inspect them. Check the bearings. Are the balls worn or

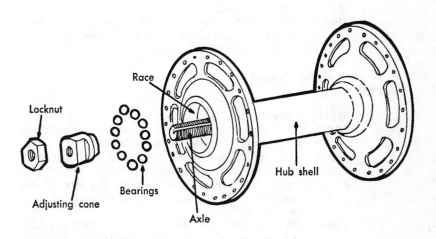

FIGURE 41

pitted? Examine the surface where the balls race—maybe in the hub, as in Figure 41, or the bearing cups, as in Figure 42. Look at all threaded parts and try them for stripped or botched threads.

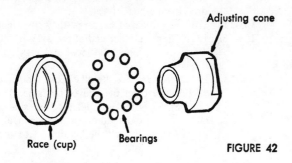

Adjusting cone

Race (cup)   Bearings

FIGURE 42

10J-15. Place the axle on a flat surface and slowly roll it to be sure it's not bent.

10J-16. Make sure dust caps and bearing cages aren't bent. Bent parts in hubs can sometimes be straightened. Worn parts should be replaced.

Putting it all back together is a snap. Remember a few keys:

10K-1. Grease the bearings and race surfaces.

10K-2. If the unit has loose balls, be sure the dust caps are tapped down squarely in place all the way around.

10K-3. After axle, bearings, cone, and locknut are positioned in the hub on one side, be careful to hold it in place until the unit is resting on the towel again. If it slips out, you may have to take time out to find the ball that rolled under the workbench.

10K-4. When you turn down the second cone, tighten it fully, and then back off about ⅛ of a turn. Hold the cone with one wrench while tightening the locknut against its washer.

Now if everything is back right, you can hold one locknut and see if the wheel can be moved side to side and if the axle turns without binding. Side-to-side movement means tighten the cone ever so

66

slightly; a binding axle means loosen. Just loosen the locknut, adjust, and try again.

When it's adjusted, it's ready to go back on the fork.

Rear hubs for derailleur-equipped bikes will be almost the same, the big difference being that you'll have to remove a freewheel cluster or sprocket and sometimes a spoke protector. See Chapter 13 for this. The key to putting all back together is to put the right side together first, so you adjust the cone from the left side.

Now that you know all about hubs, remember to try adjusting the cones to correct a problem before you take the hub all apart.

11
Frames, Forks, and Headsets

Frame

Since the frame has no moving parts, it's easy to maintain. But since it holds the entire vehicle together to make it a bike, it's important.

In most cases, all you have to worry about is the finish. We already know from the TLC table how to care for this. If it needs painting, we'll get to that in a minute.

Some time you may get tagged by a speeding tree or otherwise damage the frame. A break can be welded—but usually even the best welding jobs don't turn out super.

If a frame is bent, it can sometimes be straightened. You'll note that the diagram (Figure 43) showing the frame nomenclature refers to several of the mem-

FIGURE 43

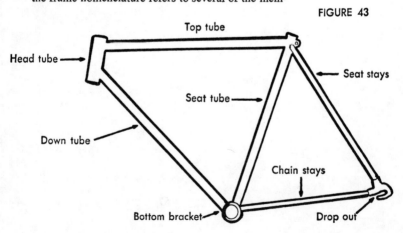

the frame nomenclature refers to several of the members as "tubes." They are hollow tubes, and as such can't easily be hammered straight. Usually, pressure from a sort of tourniquet arrangement will be the

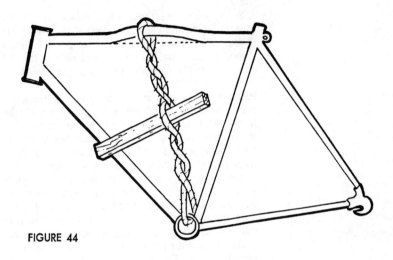

FIGURE 44

best course to take. (See Figure 44.) Remember to set the pulling rope on the center of the bend and at right angles to the tube. This kind of straightening takes days and may have to be done in steps, turning the crank a little each day. After you've taken the pressure off, check to see if it's straight. If not, you'll have to apply the tourniquet again.

If the drop outs get bent, you can tap or pry to try to get them back the way they should be.

Spreading or tourniquet-type pressure can sometimes realign the rear fork arms (chain stay and seat stay) if they aren't the correct distance apart. Sometimes an extra washer is better than trying to bring the arms back together.

"OK Al," you're saying, "You sure don't sound very sure about this frame fixin'!" You're right. Once tubular metal has been bent, it's difficult to straighten,

69

and even if it looks straight, the stretching it suffered when bent leaves a weak point that is probably going to bend again.

Welding may or may not permanently mend a break, and the bike is going to require repainting. Consider that along with the cost of repairing the frame.

Sorry, gang, but those are the facts of life on frames. Try to straighten, but don't slash your wrists if you can't. If you decide to replace, see if there's a good second-hand frame that will replace the old one. Better still, look out for those speeding trees!

Painting • The proper way to repaint the frame on your bike is to completely strip everything off the frame. And, maybe you've figured this out—*after the painting is done, the whole thing has to be put back together again.* This should make you think twice before you decide to paint. The best solution to the cosmetology of your bike is to take care of it so it won't need new paint. The original paint job on most bikes is baked on and is a good one. Protect it. If and when it gets scratches, touch it up to prevent rust and further paint loss. Some bike manufacturers put out paint sticks that exactly match their various colors. The scratch is covered by rubbing over with the paint stick and then buffing with a rag. Others put out small bottles of matching touch-up paint. The regular waxing we suggested earlier is a giant step toward protecting the finish.

If you do repaint, use acrylic enamel spray paint. If you'll get this from a bike shop, the can will be just about the right amount. Follow the instructions!

You can also buy decals with the brand and model name for many bikes, as well as decorative decals.

--------------------------------- **Fork Assembly**

The fork assembly is your bike's steering mechanism and includes the fork itself, plus the handlebars, stem, and headset. In this section we'll cover each of these components except for handlebars which we learned about in Chapter 9. They're relatively simple, but vital to your safety and cycling pleasure.

Fork • As you can see in Figure 45, the fork is the kind of part that doesn't get out of whack without your doing something to cause it—like running into a tree or leaving it out to be run over by a Mack truck. A bent fork is a little easier to straighten than a bent frame. But here again, the fork may or may not be completely cured when you're through.

The quick way is to find a length of pipe that will fit over the bent prong. Remove the wheel. Using all your strength and a few bicycle terms not found in the Glossary, bend it back as near as possible to its original shape.

The slow method is to use a tourniquet as shown.

If you've been unsuccessful at the fork straightening, or if it looks as if you'll never be able to do it, take it to your bike repairman. If he cares, he'll tell you whether it's worth straightening, and if so, will do the job.

As you can see, I have the same confidence on straightening forks as I had on frames. Try it, and hope it works. If not, get a new one.

Stem • Many years ago I was told to check my bike from "stem to stern." I've finally found out where the stem is, but I'm still searching for the stern. (Probably a foreign name for the pedal.) The stem, or gooseneck, comes in several styles, but they all have the same basic components as shown.

Very little can go wrong with the stem. It can get loose, which means you lose steering control. This is easy to remedy. Probably all it needs is to tighten the expander bolt. If it won't stay tight, then something is wrong inside, and you'll have to remove the stem.

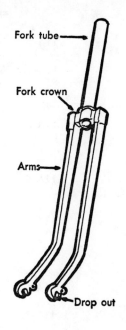

FIGURE 45

FIGURE 46

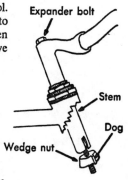

11A-1. Naturally, if you have gear levers attached to the stem, take 'em off.

11A-2. You may eventually have to take the handlebars off if, when you get inside, you find the stem must be replaced. If you want to do that now, loosen the clamp or binder bolt.

11A-3. Any accessories on the handlebar will have to be removed from one side. This will usually have to include tape and end plug if the handlebar is wrapped, or the grip if it's not.

11A-4. Now pull the bar through the clamp. If you don't need the handlebars off, you can see it's better to leave them attached to the stem.

11A-5. To remove the stem, turn the expander bolt two or three turns counterclockwise. This will cause the bolt to rise up a little. Place a scrap of wood over it and tap it down. This forces the wedge nut or taper plug to unseat from the stem.

11A-6. Straddle the front wheel to hold it steady. Grab the stem and pull upward as you twist it back and forth. It's out!

11A-7. If you don't see the taper plug (also called expander cone) at the bottom, you turned the bolt too much. Turn the bike upside down, and it'll fall out.

11A-8. Check the stem to see if it's cracked. This can happen at the slot, or if there's no slot, at the bottom. (Stems can also get cracked at the clamp where the handlebar goes, but you would already have spotted that from out side.)

11A-9. Examine the threads on the bolt and plug. If it's a slotted stem, the plug will have a lug or a ridge. Make sure it hasn't been chewed up.

11A-10. Should you find any of these flaws, replace the part. If the stem needs replacing, make sure you get one with a clamp the right size for your handlebars.

RULE OF THUMB: *In replacing the stem, at least 2½ inches of the stem must be down in the headset.*

To replace the stem:

11B-1. Make sure the plug lug is lined up with the stem slot.

11B-2. To start tightening the expander and make sure the plug lug stays in place, pull upward as you turn it with your fingers.

11B-3. Before you tighten the expander bolt completely, make sure the handlebars are at right angles to the wheel.

11B-4. After the expander bolt is tightened, test the handlebars with your hands to be sure nothing slips.

FIGURE 47

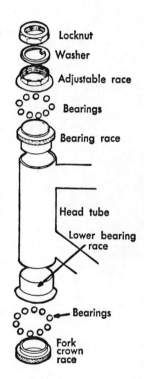

Locknut

Washer

Adjustable race

Bearings

Bearing race

Head tube

Lower bearing race

Bearings

Fork crown race

Headset • The headset includes all those parts shown in Figure 47. They hold the fork to the head tube. These parts also allow the fork to turn inside.

There are headset problems that can be corrected by mere adjustment. If the fork is loose in the headset, you can probably adjust. To adjust, loosen the locknut (Figure 47), and loosen the adjusting cup or race. Now turn it tight with your hand. The fork should no longer be loose. If it is, tighten it about another ⅛ turn.

If the fork seems to bind when turning, the adjusting race needs to be slightly loosened.

Should these adjustments not correct the problem, you'll need to take the headset apart.

The headset shown is typical, but there are variations—most of which are in the form of different types of bearings. Some will have loose bearings, while others will be caged. Some will have two rows of bearings in each cage. Still others will have top and bottom bearings that are different from each other.

It's a good idea to string the parts on a wire or make a diagram to be sure you get them all back in the right order. OK, let's take it apart.

You have to remove the stem, and if you've read the first part of this chapter you know how that's done.

11C-1. Place the bike over on its side with a clean white T-shirt underneath. (A rag or towel will do, but a greasy T-shirt makes you look more like a professional mechanic.)

11C-2. Place it on the left side if you're right handed, and vice versa if you're a southpaw.

11C-3. Remove the locknut and the keyed washer under it. If you have Huret Sprint selector levers, they'll be attached under the locknut too. Or if you have center-pull brakes, the cable hanger will be under the washer.

11C-4. Loosen the adjusting cup. Before you take it completely off, grab the down tube with your left hand (if you're right handed), and hook your thumb under the fork. This will hold the fork up tight in the head tube and keep the parts from scattering in eighty-seven directions. Now you see why you had to lay it over on a particular side. This leaves your working hand free to work.

11C-5. Remove the adjustable cup. Take it slow because there may be loose balls ready to spring out. If so, count them as they fall on your white T-shirt.

11C-6. Now you can slowly extract the fork from its head tube and catch the bottom ball bearings if they're loose. In case they're different, it's a good idea to keep upper and lower bearings separate.

11C-7. The next parts in my diagram and probably in your headset are the upper and lower set-bearing cones or races. You notice they are still stuck in the head tube (or should be). They are made to fit tightly and stay. Inspect them for bends, wear, and pitted places. Also see that they are squarely seated in the head tube. If everything is A-OK, leave 'em alone. If they are not squarely seated, place a block of wood against the end and tap until it seats. If these cones are damaged, you'll have to replace 'em. The best way to remove one is with a hardwood stick. Place the stick into the other end of the head tube against the lip of the set cone as shown in Figure 48. Tap gently with

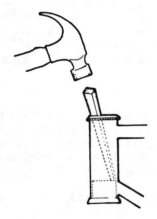

FIGURE 48

a hammer, moving the stick around the lip as you go. When it's out, take it with you to be sure you get an exact replacement.

11C-8. If both cups have to be removed, make a note of which is top and which is bottom. The bottom part in the typical headset is the fork crown race, and it's still on the fork. If something is wrong with it, a small screwdriver will pry it off. Take it slow and work all around the part.

11C-9. Check over all the bearings, cups, and cones for wear or pitting. If everything checks out, give all the parts a good toothbrushing in solvent. Check 'em again after they're clean. Sometimes a flaw is hidden by grease.

Want to get it all back together?

11D-1. Run a rag through the head tube to clean it out.

11D-2. If you had to remove the set-bearing cones, replace these using the tap-and-block method to seat them squarely.

11D-3. If you had to remove the fork crown race, tap it gently back into place. Use the wood block here too.

11D-4. Grease the lower bearings if they're caged, and slip them over the fork tube and in place in the race. If not, put grease in both the fork crown race and the lower set-bearing cone. Place the loose balls in the grease in the fork race. Be sure you got them all back in. Don't just look to see if there are any left, count 'em.

11D-5. With bearings in place, insert the fork tube into the head tube.

11D-6. Hold it firmly in place, and with the bike upright, place the top bearings in the top bearing cone. Use the same lubricating procedures as on the bottom bearings.

11D-7. Keep holding the fork tight. Now slip the adjusting race over the fork tube and screw it in place. Use the same adjusting process we described earlier. Now you can let go of the fork.

Check now to see if the fork is firmly set in place, and if it turns easily. If so, put all that other good stuff back in place. If not, adjust, check your work, and get it right.

75

12

Brakes

Basically, there are only two types of brakes on bicycles. The coaster brake is activated by pushing either pedal backward. When this is done, the brake, located inside the rear hub assembly, takes hold and stops the bike. The other type of brake is the hand brake, or caliper brake. This is by far the most popular these days, and with derailleur gears, it's the only way to go—er, stop.

Coaster Brakes

All the bikes back in my day had coaster brakes. Most of the 1- and 3-speed machines of today have this type of stopping mechanism. The tip-off is that there are no brake levers on the handlebars. Also, coaster brakes require a brake arm (Figure 49). The brake is located inside the rear hub and is applied by pushing the foot against the pedal as if to reverse pedal. When you are pedaling forward, the sprocket turns and engages to cause the back wheel to turn. When you coast, the sprocket disengages, but the wheel continues its turning. When you push

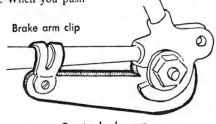

Brake arm clip

FIGURE 49

Coaster brake arm

backward, another clutch engages, and the wheel is stopped from turning. The brake arm we mentioned keeps the wheel from turning after the brake inside the hub is engaged. Whether there are shoes, teeth, a cylinder, or discs that act as brakes, the general principle of coaster brakes is the same.

Maybe a look inside will help. The parts in Figure 51 are all spread out in order. This particular brake has a cylinder that is expanded against the hub shell to cause the bike to stop. Starting over at the far right, you can see how the sprocket can engage either the driving business or the braking business. When the sprocket says "stop," the brake cone goes to work to do its thing with the cylinder.

FIGURE 50

But that's enough of this highly technical chatter. There are many things that will apply to most any kind of coaster brake. After we've covered these, we'll talk a little bit about some of the different and most popular kinds, hopefully the kind you have. If you aren't really that much of a do-it-yourself mechanic, go slow about tackling actual coaster brake repairs. This is a fairly complicated little part of your bike—and I might add, one that must work for your safety.

Maybe your trouble will only require lubrication, adjustment, or the replacement of an obvious part. First, let's talk about lubrication.

You will remember that bearings require light grease, so if you're going to oil in through the oiler cap (if your bike has one, see Figure 50), don't use the lightweight household machine oil we've recommended for so many other parts. This would tend to dissolve the grease that has been packed around the bearings. A medium-weight motor oil, such as SAE 30, is about right. If you don't have the oiler cap, squirt the oil in at each side and turn the pedals forward and apply the brakes to get the oil to reach all the parts. Above all, don't over-oil!

After a while, the bearings will need a grease job. Probably every six months for the active cycler. So why not just give it a grease job? It's not that simple. You have to take the whole thing apart. That's not so bad, but then, you have to get it back together—in the proper order—and properly adjusted. Don't worry. You can do it!

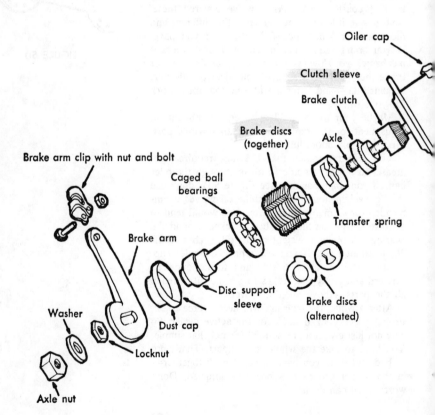

Oiler cap

Clutch sleeve

Brake clutch

Brake discs
(together)

Axle

Brake arm clip with nut and bolt

Caged ball
bearings

Transfer spring

Brake arm

Disc support
sleeve

Brake discs
(alternated)

Washer

Dust cap

Locknut

Axle nut

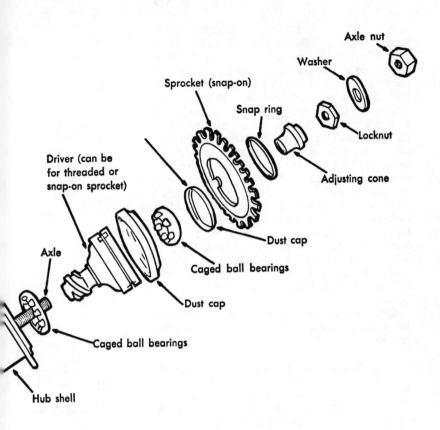

Axle nut

Washer

Sprocket (snap-on)

Snap ring

Locknut

Adjusting cone

Driver (can be for threaded or snap-on sprocket)

Axle

Dust cap

Caged ball bearings

Dust cap

Caged ball bearings

Hub shell

FIGURE 51

New Departure Type Coaster Brake

First, look at the several types of exploded rear hubs. If yours isn't shown, you will need to know what differences there are in the parts yours has. Make a large rough sketch of the order of the parts on the one that you think will be the closest to yours. As you take each part off, check with the sketch. Note any differences. Another trick is to string the parts on a wire to keep them in order. As you take each part off, drop it into a container of solvent. As long as it has to come apart anyway, you may as well clean all the parts. Take a small brush and really give each part a good scrubbing. After they are clean, spread them out on a paper towel to dry. Inspect each part for wear. A small worn or broken part should be replaced. However, you may have to shop around to find a dealer who stocks parts for your particular kind. In fact, he may have to order them. The good guys will do this. After the solvent has dried, pack light grease around the bearings. The best kind comes in a tube from the bike shop and is especially for coaster brakes.

Specifically, let's overhaul a New Departure coaster brake. As you can see, this system employs a series of discs.

12A-1.	Start with the wheel off (Procedure 10F) and preferably with the left end of the axle in a vise (crunch!). This means the sprocket is aimed up.
12A-2.	Loosen the locknut. It works best if you use two wrenches and hold the cone with one.
12A-3.	With this off, you can now unscrew the cone. Be sure to note any washers and their sequence.
12A-4.	The sprocket will probably have a snap-on spring clip. A screwdriver will flip it off. Before you flip though, turn the sprocket to start unscrewing the driver. Once the spring clip is off, lift the sprocket off.
12A-5.	The sprocket will have a dust cap and caged bearings fitted in the lip. Remove this by prying up on the dust cap—slow and easy so as not to bend it.
12A-6.	Now finish unscrewing the driver unit.
12A-7.	Once it's out of the way, the unit comes out of the hub shell when you lift the wheel up.
12A-8.	Next, there's another caged bearing to lift off.
12A-9.	You'll then come to the clutch assembly which includes

80

a sleeve, the clutch, and a transfer spring. Slide them up off the axle.

12A-10. Now you can lift up the discs. Grab the bottom one so they'll all come up as a unit. IMPORTANT: Disc systems will often have different-shaped discs. Check the sequence. Usually there'll be two different-shaped discs that alternate. Also, count to be sure you get them all back in.

12A-11. Remove the next caged bearing.

12A-12. If the race on the disc support sleeve is not worn or pitted, you can just leave it on the axle.

12A-13. The clutch assembly that you removed comes apart. The sleeve pulls out of the transfer spring, and the clutch turns out of the spring.

All the parts go into solvent for a good cleaning and inspection. Right now, you're probably wondering how you'll ever get all those parts back in that small hub. Don't worry; most of 'em can be crammed back.

See if any of the bearings are worn or pitted. Make sure their cages aren't bent. See that the races are OK.

Inspect all threaded parts to see that none have been stripped.

Check the teeth in the clutch parts.

Examine each disc for wear or damage.

Replace any bad parts. Take the bad part along to get a match. Some of the parts of coaster brake systems from one manufacturer are interchangeable with other makes. Your cycle-analyst can tell you which will and which won't.

Before you start cramming the parts back in, slick 'em up. Grease the bearings, the races, the clutch, and the inside of the hub shell. Pour a little oil—30w is about right—into a jar lid and put the discs in.

Brake discs (alternated)

FIGURE 52

Putting it back together is pretty much a reverse process to disassembly. Remember to be sure to get the discs back in the right order. Also, some of the discs will have lugs (Figure 52). Line these up with some sort of straight edge.

Don't forget that the two large caged bearings face each other with flat sides out. The small bearing at the sprocket has the flat side out too. Be sure the sprocket has the same side out as it did originally.

We've already mentioned the importance of getting everything back in the proper order. Of equal import is to get the bearings back in facing the same way they came out.

> RULE OF THUMB: *The balls fit against the cone-shaped part with the cage facing out from it.*

The next step is to adjust the bearings against the cones so that they have the proper clearance. The key to this is an adjusting cone that you'll see in most of the exploded views of the different hubs. When this is adjusted properly, the axle should turn easily, but without any play. Then when it's properly set, a locknut goes on to keep it from getting out of whack. If it's not right, undo the locknut and readjust.

When you get to the adjusting cone, turn it down finger tight, and then back off ¼ of a turn. With the left end of the axle in a vise, hold the cone with one wrench and tighten the locknut down with another.

If there's any end-to-end movement of the hub in the shell, loosen the locknut and tighten the cone ever so slightly—maybe no more than ¹⁄₃₂ of a turn.

Now put the wheel back on and make sure the brake arm is securely held to the left chain stay. You should be able to stop on a dime, and get nine cents change.

Figure 53 is typical of coaster brake shoes. Only the shoes and expanders are shown because most of the other parts are like the disc system (Figure 50).

Here again, your bike may be a little different, so keep close track of the parts and note differences so you can get it back right.

Shoes

Brake shoes and expanders

FIGURE 53

12B-1. With the wheel off (see Procedure 10F), start by removing the right locknut. It will come off best if you put the left end of the axle in a vise and hold the cone with one wrench while you loosen the locknut with the other.

12B-2. There'll be a washer or two before you come to the cone. You'll probably be able to get it off with your fingers.

12B-3. Next, turn the sprocket. It will extract the drive unit.

12B-4. The sprocket can now be separated from the driver. Do you see the snap ring clip? Pry it up and off.

12B-5. Back to the axle—lift out the caged ball bearings.

12B-6. Now the unit can come out of its shell. Just lift the wheel up, but do it slowly. The two brake shoes are going to fall out. You'll want to catch them before they fall into your own shoes. (Used to be, you could depend on small parts falling in your cuffs, but with no cuffs . . .)

12B-7. Next lift off the clutch assembly. It comes apart by just pulling the driver clutch from the retarder spring.

12B-8. This leaves the brake expander and brake arm. To remove these, take the axle out of the vise, remove the locknut, slide the arm, maybe a washer, a dust cap, and caged bearings, and you can screw the expander unit off the axle.

It's a temptation to take up roller skating! But don't worry, you'll get it back together.

Now it's time to brush all parts clean and have an inspection. Look for bearings that are pitted or worn.

Check the races for the same problems.

Be sure the cages aren't bent.

Study the threaded parts to be certain they aren't stripped.

The clutch has serrated edges, and these sometimes wear smooth.

Make a survey of the shoes. If there's been a lack of lubrication, they may be worn smooth. Replace them.

See that the retarder spring hasn't sprung.

Inspect all other surfaces for wear, breakage, or rust.

With all the parts cleaned or replaced, you'll do well to lube everything as you put it back together. (Sure, it'll go back together.) Light grease for the ball bearings, the hub shell, the brake shoes, the retarder spring, and the clutch face—and a medium-weight oil (30w) for the rest.

Putting it back together is pretty much a reversal of the disassembly. There are a few hints to make it easier and better.

The expander unit needs to be turned on the axle, leaving about 1¼ inches of threads sticking out.

Line up the raised lugs on both the expander and

the retarder units when the clutch assembly is slid in place on the axle.

With the shoes seated in place against the lugs, hold the unit by the shoes to keep it intact while inserting it in the hub shell.

When it comes to turning the cone down against the sprocket, screw it on finger tight. Then back it up ¼ of a turn.

Use a wrench to hold the cone while you tighten the locknut.

Once you've gotten this done, test to be sure that the wheel will turn freely and that there's only the slightest end-to-end play in the axle. If it won't turn freely, loosen the locknut and loosen the cone a tiny bit. If there's excess end-to-end movement, tighten the cone. Get this right before you put the wheel back on.

Other models, including those with brake cylinders, come apart and go back pretty much the same way. On some, the driver unit and the axle are all one.

Another variation is the type that has a squared end on the right side of the axle. The "innards" are about the same, but this is for adjustment. With the brake arm held firm, the axle is turned until it pulls the unit tight. Then back off a quarter-turn and tighten the locknut on the arm side.

Since there are so many, many different coaster-brake units, we'd need an extra volume to cover them all. If you'll read all the foregoing, you'll be confused, but you'll be able to overhaul your coaster brake hub.

Caliper Brakes

Caliper brakes are currently by far the most popular—with both cyclers and writers. It's a lot easier to tell all about these hand brakes than those complicated coaster jobs. There are two basic types: the side-pull and the center-pull. They stop you by applying brake shoes or pads against the rims. Most bikes will have these hand brakes both front and back.

There are actually three separate units to the caliper brake system: the lever, the cable, and the brake mechanism. If you have a problem, try to ascertain which of the three units is responsible.

First, go over this quickie checklist (look at the drawings to see exactly which part we're talking about):

12C-1. Check the cable (Figure 54) to be sure there aren't any kinks or frayed places.

12C-2. Inspect the housings for the same things.

12C-3. Test the brake levers to see that they work and release properly and to be sure they aren't either bent or broken.

12C-4. Check the shoes or rubber pads for wear. Also check to be sure the rubber is still live.

12C-5. Make sure the rims aren't bent. A rough spot can foul up the proper workings of the brakes. Also, check the wheel to be sure it's in alignment. If the wheel wobbles, ture it by following the instructions starting on page 58.

12C-6. Apply the brakes and see that the shoes both touch the rim at the same time. When released, they should be the same distance from the rim. If not, you'll learn how to adjust them a little later in this chapter.

12C-7. Make sure the shoes don't touch the tire. This makes for bad braking and also wears out tires rather rapidly.

If the brakes are just sticky, it's easy to isolate the part that is sticking. First, check the caliper mechanism. Squeeze the shoes with your fingers. Let go, and they should snap back in place. With brake shoes again held in place against the rim, see if the hand lever will move back and forth smoothly. Release the cable at the mechanism (see the how-to part later in this chapter). Pull the end of the cable and have the lever squeezed. When the lever is released, you should be able to easily pull the cable back. Once isolated, you can go to the section on the particular part and take care of it.

Adjusting the Brakes • If everything else checks out, the brakes can now be adjusted—if needed. To find out if they need this, measure to see that the brake shoes are about ⅛ inch from the rim. If not, a simple adjustment will correct it.

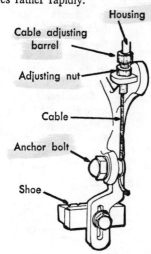

FIGURE 54

85

12D-1. If there is an adjusting nut at the end of the cable hous ing, as shown in Figure 54, you're in business. Loosen the adjusting nut.

12D-2. Next, turn the adjusting barrel counterclockwise. This will move the shoes in toward the rim. They never need to be moved out—well, hardly ever. If you're a "hardly ever," turn it clockwise.

12D-3. When the ⅛ inch is reached, turn the adjusting nut back down tight.

If you don't have an adjusting barrel or if the shoes are so far away from the rim that the adjusting barrel won't cut it, here's what to do.

12E-1. Clamp the shoes against the rim with your hand. (That "third hand" tool is quite handy here!)

12E-2. Loosen the cable anchor bolt.

12E-3. Grab the end of the cable and pull it tight.

12E-4. Retighten the anchor bolt.

12E-5. Release the shoes and check—you may have to do it again to get it right on the ⅛-inch mark.

Brake Hand Levers

Although caliper brakes have several different-looking hand levers made by many different companies, they operate pretty much the same. Probably the biggest difference is in the way they are attached to the handlebars. There are also minor variations in the way the cable attaches to the lever.

Some levers attach by a clamp with outside bolts, as in Figure 55. Many popular models have a screw that is hidden inside and can be reached only when the hand lever is held down, as in Figure 56.

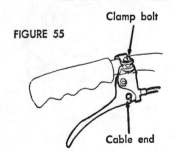

FIGURE 55

Clamp bolt

Cable end

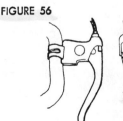

FIGURE 56

Screw or bolt that holds clamp

Cable end

With lever squeezed

If the lever is not working properly, it's probably lack of lubrication. If the lever is sticking or hard to apply, put light oil or spray WD-40 on moving parts. Work the lever back and forth to distribute the oil. If the brake lever is held in the housing by a nut and bolt instead of by an axle, it may be too tight. Set it so it doesn't bind the lever, but don't make it too loose.

If this hasn't worked, look for a bent part. The lever could be bent and binding. The housing could be bent. Try to observe the bend while the lever is on the bike and all together. You may even be able to straighten a bend without taking the unit apart.

If you have to dismantle:

12F-1. Remove the tape if your bars are wrapped.

12F-2. Next, hold the brake pads against the rim. Here's where that "third hand" we mentioned comes in handy.

12F-3. Release the cable tension. If you have a quick-release mechanism, that does it. Otherwise, move ahead to the section on brake units. Find your kind of calipers and see how it's done. Don't pull the cable all the way out at the caliper unit if you've had to loosen it there.

12F-4. The cable will fit in a slot in the lever (Figure 55 or 56), and when the tension is gone, it slips out easily.

12F-5. If the unit is held on the handlebars by an outside clamp, undo it.

12F-6. The lever will probably be held in the housing by a nut and bolt. By removing this, the whole shebang falls apart. Check to be sure the axle on which the lever moves isn't bent or scored to keep the lever from working.

12F-7. If your lever is the kind with a bolt inside, as in Figure 56, squeeze the lever, and you can get at the bolt. When it's undone, the entire unit comes apart.

To straighten a lever or housing, take it easy. Try to do it with your hands if possible. If you have to resort to tools, cover the metal tool or part with masking tape to prevent a botch-up. If it won't straighten, get a new part. Most shops will have most parts for most brakes.

On the models held by an outside bolt, getting it back together is a snap. The other kind requires patience, but it can be done. With either kind, be sure to position the lever right for your hand and be sure it's clamped on good and tight so it won't slip.

All the foregoing is applicable to either a right- or a left-hand lever.

Side-Pull Calipers

While there are many different makes of side-pull units, they're all very much alike. The exploded view in Figure 57 is fairly typical. If it's not exactly like yours, sketch out the difference so you'll be sure to get all the parts back in the right sequence. One washer out of place can throw the works off—which may throw you off the bike.

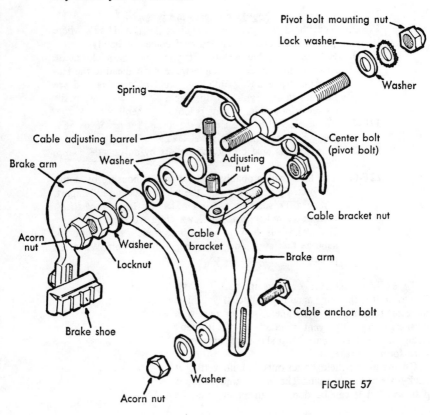

FIGURE 57

If you've tried the adjustments previously mentioned, and have convinced yourself that overhaul is the only answer, here's how to get a brake torn down so it's in as many parts as shown in Figure 57.

12G-1. Loosen the acorn nut that holds the cable anchor bolt and remove the cable. The cable will pull right out. It's a good idea to tape the cable end to a convenient part of the frame so it doesn't get smashed.

12G-2. Remove the nut on the opposite side of the frame from the unit and collect all the washers, spacers, and other doodads. Keep 'em in order.

12G-3. The unit will now come off.

12G-4. Take a small screwdriver and pry up the ends of the spring. Be careful, because when it gets loose from the stop on the arm, it will try to straighten out at the end to stab your finger.

12G-5. Remove the acorn nut, the locknut, and the washer(s).

12G-6. Now the arms and all that other good stuff will slide right off the center bolt.

Are you keeping track of how it all goes back? If you're sure you know the order, let it all come apart and into the solvent (all except the pads). Cleanliness is next to goodliness for caliper parts. After everything is clean and dry, look it over for worn or bent parts.

RULE OF THUMB: *With brakes, 'tis better to replace than repair.*

In reinstalling, reverse the order. Hand tighten the locknut before tightening the acorn nut down. Now, you remember how that spring tried to stab you when you took it off? It's going to fight you some more. Hook one end of the spring on the inner arm, and then grab the other end of the spring with pliers and ease it over the stop on the other arm.

Put the unit back on, reattach the cable, oil the pivot points, and adjust as previously described.

89

Center-Pull Units

Here again, lots of people make 'em, and I've exploded a typical unit in Figure 58. Check yours for differences and sketch them out.

Adjusting didn't do it here, so an overhaul is your next step.

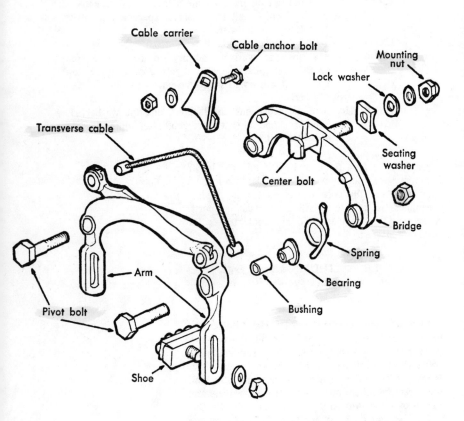

FIGURE 58

12H-1. You will need to release the cable carrier from the cable, and this is done by loosening the nut that holds it. Remove the transverse cable. It will most likely be connected to the brake arms in one of the two ways shown in Figures 59 and 60.

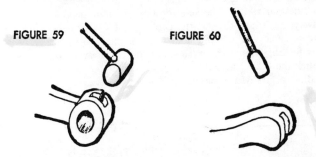

FIGURE 59   FIGURE 60

12H-2. On the side of the frame opposite the unit, there will be a mounting nut. Take it—and whatever else is on the post —off. Keep track of the sequence.

12H-3. Now the entire unit will slip off.

12H-4. The two springs can be pried off by slipping a small screwdriver under the exposed end of each and lifting over the stop.

12H-5. Next you can undo the two pivot bolts.

12H-6. As you can see from my exploded view, this will release a whole bunch of little parts.

12H-7. Some units have poles from the bridge for the arms to pivot on. If your unit is different, be doubly sure to keep track of the order. When you take the springs out, tie a wire around the right one because they are *not* interchangeable.

Dump all the parts except the pads into solvent and clean 'em well. Dry and carefully examine each part for wear, bends, or cracks. Replace any bad parts.

Start your reassembly by placing the spring loops on the bridge, making sure you remove the wire that told you the right from the left. Place all the bushings, spacers, bearings, and whatever back on the pivot bolts and fasten the arms to the bridge. Be sure you get them all in the right order. Lightly oil all the pivot points and see that they move smoothly.

Now is the point where many will earn a Purple Heart—slipping the springs back in place over the stops. The best way I've found is to pry the end over the stop with a screwdriver. The ends of these springs are too short to grab with pliers as you can do with a side-pull spring. The screwdriver gets your hand away. Patience! Reinsert the two ends of the transverse cable and put the unit back in place on the frame. Slip the transverse cable over the cable carrier. Stick the brake cable into the cable anchor bolt and adjust as previously described.

Caliper Parts

Each part for either kind of caliper brake can be bought separately. However, all shops aren't going to carry all parts. It's good to check with your favorite shop to see just what you can get in case you need it. It may make a difference in whether you'll try to straighten bolts or smooth out pivot posts with steel wool. The parts are inexpensive, so new ones are preferable.

Shoes

If the rubber pads on brake shoes are worn or have become hardened, then baby needs a new pair of shoes. And when one is damaged, you might just as well get all new ones.

Before you remove them, however, they may have a message for you. Look at how the wear is. If it's uneven, it can show that the brakes were not properly aligned. If the pad on one side is worn and the other is not, it means that either only one pad was hitting the rim or there's a rim flaw. When they've told you all they can, remove them.

Brake shoes are attached in two ways: the threaded stud type (Figure 61) and the eye bolt type (Figure 62). Either way, they come off by undoing one nut.

If the metal holder is OK, you can replace the pads only. There is an open end to the holder, and the pad can be driven out, and a new one driven in.

FIGURE 61

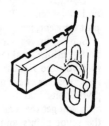

FIGURE 62

Some people end up bending the holder while knocking the pad in or out—so be careful. When you've got 'em in, reinstall on the calipers.

> RULE OF THUMB: *Always install brake shoes with the closed end of the holder facing forward. Otherwise, when you put on the brakes, the rim will force the pad out.*

Adjust the shoes as already described, and you're all done.

Brake Cables

If your cable has become frayed any place other than the end that sticks out, replace it. It's easy to do. First, remove the old cable.

12I-1. Loosen the cable anchor bolt (see Figure 54).
12I-2. Pull the cable out of its anchor.
12I-3. Press the hand lever which will expose the cable end. It should be one of the two types in Figures 55 or 56. Remove it from its slot.
12I-4. Pull the cable out.

Now would be an excellent time to check the housings to be sure they're still OK. If they are kinked or if the ferrules are botched, you should take the old cable to your cycle-analyst to be sure you get an exact match—except unfrayed.

Putting the cable back in is a snap. Lightly lubricate it and start at the lever. As you thread it through the housing, twist it as you push it through. Twist in the opposite way to which it was wound at the factory. This keeps the end of a strand from catching on anything as it goes through.

When the cable is again in the anchor, tighten the anchor nut and adjust as previously described.

> RULE OF THUMB: *Never snip off excess cable until the cable is back in and adjusted.*

93

13

Pedals, Cranks,
and Sprockets

There are dozens of different styles of pedals, but
the most popular are (1) the old-style rubber-tread
pedal and (2) the all-metal, or rattrap, pedal. Bike
purists will use nothing but the rattrap with a toe
clip. If you ever cycle barefooted, you'll be a member
of the rubber-tread cult. On the other hand (or foot),
if your wet sneakers have slipped off the rubber-
treads while you're straining up a hill—well, decide
for yourself.

The anatomy of both types of pedals is the same.
The rattrap (Figure 63) is usually a one-piece platform. Rubber-treads are removable, as shown in
Figure 64. All you have to do is remove the nuts
on the inner side, and the frame and treads come
off.

After the frame is off, if you are going to take
the pedal apart for lubrication:

13A-1.   Remove the locknut counterclockwise.
13A-2.   Unscrew the bearing cone counterclockwise.

Now all the other parts in Figure 64 will slide off
the spindle.

While you've got it apart, clean everything in
solvent and check for worn or pitted bearings,
damaged or bent ball cages, rough spindle, stripped
threads, or worn races. All these parts are available
at a well-stocked bike shop, but if you can't find the

94

part you need, an entire new pedal doesn't cost that
much. (Or see if there's an old bike in the neighborhood that you can strip.)

In putting the whole smear back together:

13B-1. Pack the bearings with grease.

13B-2. Put all the parts back together in the reverse order of their removal. (Remember the bearing retainers go into the cups with the ball side against the cup.)

13B-3. Now screw the cone back on the spindle. When it is down all the way, back it up slightly counterclockwise about ⅛ turn.

13B-4. Add the key washer and locknut, and tighten the nut clockwise down completely.

13B-5. Now the spindle housing should turn easily. If not, the cone must be backed up again—maybe another ⅛ turn. If there is any wobble to the side, the cone is loose and must be turned clockwise.

13B-6. The frame now goes back on, and when you spin the pedal, it should purr.

Rattraps differ:

13C-1. They have a dust cap (Figure 63) that usually unscrews. If there's no knurled or flat surface to use a wrench on, then the dust cap pries off with a screwdriver.

13C-2. The locknut and bearing cone also unscrew, but watch out! The ball bearings are not in cages like the ones above. They're all loose, and will fall out and roll all over the place. Be sure to catch and count 'em—and, if your memory is as bad as mine, write down the number.

13C-3. Before you slide the entire platform off (it's all one piece), remember that *there are loose balls at the other end.*

The same checklist applies for the rattrap as for
the rubber-treads. The only crisis on rattraps is
getting the loose balls back in place. This is best
done with the entire pedal off the crank. (See
below.)

13D-1. Start with the end near where it connects to the crank. With the spindle in the frame, rest the other end of the frame on a surface and hold the spindle up about 2 inches

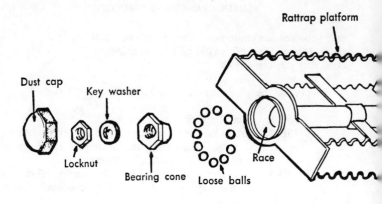

Dust cap

Key washer

Locknut

Bearing cone

Loose balls

Race

Rattrap platform

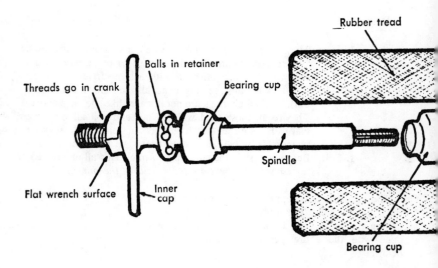

Threads go in crank

Balls in retainer

Bearing cup

Rubber tread

Flat wrench surface

Inner cap

Spindle

Bearing cup

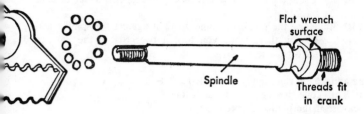

Flat wrench surface

Spindle

Threads fit in crank

FIGURE 63

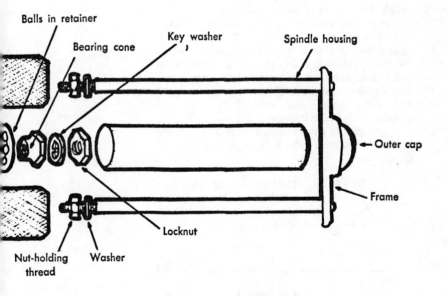

Balls in retainer

Bearing cone

Key washer

Spindle housing

Outer cap

Frame

Locknut

Nut-holding thread

Washer

FIGURE 64

from the frame to expose the cup or race in which the balls fit.

13D-2. Put grease in here.

13D-3. Using a pair of tweezers, place the proper number of balls back in.

13D-4. Raise the platform frame up tight against the spindle and keep it there while you turn it over to put the balls in the other end.

The same adjustment rules apply as on the rubber-tread jobs. The cone is the key to adjustment. Counterclockwise if the platform doesn't turn freely. Clockwise if the pedal moves sideways on its spindle.

The entire pedal can come off the crank without taking the pedal apart. You'll see a flat wrenching surface on the spindle adjacent to the crank. (It's indicated in the drawing of each type pedal.) Give the threads a few drops of penetrating oil while you look for the wrench. The only thing to remember is that the *threads are different on left and right pedals.* For the left pedal, turn clockwise to remove. To remove the right pedal, turn counterclockwise.

So you can get them back on the correct side, most pedals have an *L* or an *R* stamped somewhere on the spindle—just try to find it. Campagnola pedals have an *S* and a *D* stamped on them. These letters mean, " 'Sa de left" and "Dat'sa de right." ("Actually, sinestra and derecha," he said while glancing at his Berlitz diploma.)

If you need to buy an entire new pedal or replace a spindle, you must order by *L* or *R* and know the spindle size.

> RULE of THUMB: *Most American cranks require ½-inch spindles, and most imports use ⁹⁄₁₆-inch spindles. Better still, take the old pedal along.*

Cranks

The pedals carry your go-power to the rest of the power train by means of the crank. There are two types of cranks: the one-piece and the three-piece.

About all that can go wrong with the crank itself is that it can get bent; or if it's a three-piece, the crank can be loose on its axle.

Any attempt at straightening should be done with the crank off the bicycle. We'll get into removal next, and that will also cover the loose crank.

The bottom bracket can be loose or tight, and adjustments here will become clear as we take apart and put back the assembly.

One-piece Cranks •

FIGURE 65

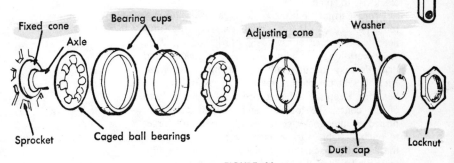

Fixed cone

Axle

Bearing cups

Adjusting cone

Washer

Sprocket

Caged ball bearings

Dust cap

Locknut

FIGURE 66

13L-1. Hold the left pedal in the left hand and loosen—do not remove—the locknut. Just as with the left pedal, removal of the left locknut requires a clockwise turn to loosen.

13E-2. With the locknut loose, remove the left pedal.

13E-3. Now go ahead and take the loc''nut completely out.

13E-4. Next off will be a keyed lock washer.

13E-5. Then you come to the adjusting cone. You should be able to remove it with your fingers. If not, see the slots in the drawing? Place a screwdriver in a slot and tap the blade with a hammer. (Don't ruin the screwdriver—just tap.) This piece also comes off clockwise, and a tap should loosen it. If not, put a few drops of penetrating oil on the thread, have a half cup of coffee, and now it comes off.

13E-6. Unlike some other parts with ball bearings, the American-made one-piece crank doesn't have loose balls. They're always caged, so you don't have to have your catcher's mitt ready. Slide the bearing off the crank and put all the loose parts in solvent.

13E-7. Now the fixed cone on the sprocket side will unseat, and the chain will come off.

13E-8. By pulling the right crank outward and tipping it toward the left crank, you can snake the crank through the bottom bracket shell and out.

13E-9. Plop the ball bearings from the right side into the solvent and start your inspection.

After brushing the parts with solvent, check the bearings to see that they are not pitted or worn. See that the cages are not bent. Inspect the cones for wear. If the right fixed cone is bad, it unscrews clockwise to come off.

I forgot to mention the cups, fixed inside the bottom bracket shell. If the bearing cups are shot, they need to be tapped out with the old hardwood stick.

If everything, including the shell, is cleaned and dry, it's easy to put it all back together. Use your stick to seat the cups. Grease them, as well as the bearings. Keep the different directions in mind. Both of the cones, the locknut, and the left pedal are turned counterclockwise to install. And don't forget to put the right bearings in place before you snake the assembly back through the shell. Also, be sure the balled side of the bearings faces the cups.

In replacing the adjusting cone, hand tighten it until there is no play from side to side. See if it turns smoothly. If not, back it up until it does, and again check the side-to-side play. Reinstall the key, washer, and locknut. Test again. If there's any play, or if it doesn't turn smoothly, loosen the locknut and adjust again. That's also how to adjust the crank even if you didn't take it apart.

Put the pedal back on the left crank arm and reinstall the chain. (See Chapter 14.)

Three-piece Cranks • The three-piece crank comes in two major varieties—the cottered and the cotterless. The overall assembly isn't that different. It's just that the crank arms are attached to the axle by different means. (Figure 67 and Figure 69.)

100

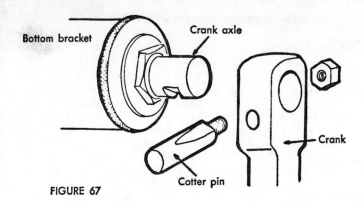

Bottom bracket   Crank axle

Crank

Cotter pin

FIGURE 67

Cottered:

13F-1. The cottered crank is removed by first unscrewing the nut.

13F-2. Cut a wood block to fit under the crank. Drill a hole in the end for the pin to fit into. Place another block over the threaded end. Strike the top block with a sharp hammer blow that is aimed straight down and at the center of the pin. Whatever you do, don't whack the pin without solid support underneath. If you don't like my block, rig up something of your own.

13F-3. With the pin out, the crank arm slides off the axle.

13F-4. On the right side, the arm and the chainwheel come off as a unit. Typically, the right crank will attach to the chainwheel by bolts. Unless the crank is bent, don't separate it from the chainwheel for this overhaul. In fact, some chainwheel-crank setups are all one piece without bolts.

FIGURE 68

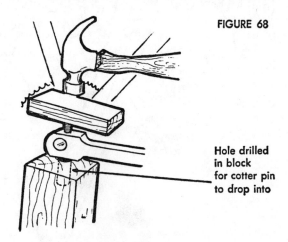

Hole drilled
in block
for cotter pin
to drop into

Cotterless: A typical cotterless crank is illustrated in Figure 69.

13G-1.   Unscrew the dust cap. If it has a slot, use a screwdriver. If it has a hex keyhole, use an Allen wrench.

13G-2.   This will reveal a bolt that is inset and almost impossible to reach. Invest a few bucks in a special tool that is made for your cotterless cranks. (See page 27.) You'll need one for adjusting too. The handle part of the crank tool reaches in and removes the bolt. The right-size metric socket wrench could do that.

13G-3.   Now, however, you really need the crank extractor part of the tool as shown. These threads go into the recently vacated dust cap threads.

13G-4.   When this is done, put the handle part on the extractor post and turn. It will go down against the axle and force the crank to back off. If stuck, remove the crank socket and tap the extractor post, and then go at it again.

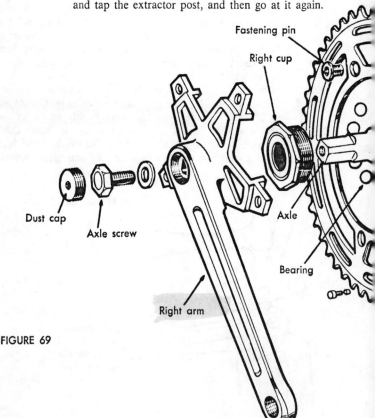

Fastening pin

Right cup

Dust cap

Axle screw

Axle

Bearing

Right arm

FIGURE 69

As mentioned earlier, the bottom bracket is much the same for either type three-piece crank, but the parts can vary slightly with different brands. Keep them in order, and either string 'em on a wire or make a diagram if you start coming up with parts different from those in Figure 69. Don't do this overhaul with the bike upside down.

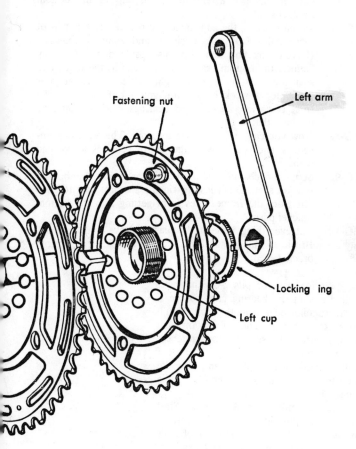

Fastening nut

Left arm

Locking ing

Left cup

13G-5. With the cranks off, start again on the left side. The first part you come to is the notched lock ring. This takes a spanner wrench, but will also come off by putting the tip of a screwdriver into a notch at an angle and tapping it counterclockwise. As soon as it moves, you can get it off with your fingers.

13G-6. Next remove the adjustable cup while holding the other end of the axle against the fixed cup in the bottom bracket shell.

13G-7. In many cases, the adjustable cup will reveal a bunch of loose balls. Do your catch-'em-and-count-'em routine. (Here's why you don't do this upside down. In many frames, the bottom bracket shell opens to the down and seat tubes. A loose ball might rattle around in your frame for a week before you got it out. Some of the three-piece jobs have caged bearings, and so you may not have that worry.)

13G-8. Now you can pull the entire axle out. The fixed cup unscrews, and you have another set of bearings to contend with.

13G-9. Some models have a plastic sleeve inside the bottom bracket shell. Don't lose it, since it's a protector to keep dirt from the frame tubes from getting into the bottom bracket parts.

13G-10. Put everything (except the plastic sleeve) into solvent. Brush all the parts clean, including inside the bottom bracket shell.

Check the balls for wear or pits. Are the cages (if any) bent? Look at the bearing cups to see if the bearings are running on a smooth track. You'll note two ridges on the axle. The outside of each ridge is a bearing surface. Be sure it's not scratched, worn, pitted, or scored.

If any of these parts needs replacement, take the bad part along to be sure you get exactly the same thing to go back in.

There's no trick to getting it back together. Start with the bike on its right side. Put light grease in the fixed cup and place the correct number of balls around the inside. If your unit had caged bearings, the exposed balls face against the cup. Now insert the axle. This is the side where the chainwheel goes, so it needs to stick out more. The end with the longest span from the ridge goes to the right. Insert the cup into the shell, using the axle to keep the bearings in place.

Did you lose the plastic sleeve? If not, put it back.

Now grease the adjustable cup and follow the same procedure with that set of bearings. Holding the right end of the axle, turn the bike over on its left side. Slip the cup over the axle and screw it back in place. Tighten it until there is no play when you push the axle back and forth from both ends. Then check to see that the axle turns freely. If not, loosen the adjusting cup. Replace the lock ring and test again. If it's out of adjustment, loosen the lock ring and get it right. (This is what you do if you only wish to adjust instead of taking the bottom bracket apart.)

The cranks go back on easily. For cottered cranks, you again need the wood block or some sort of support. The flat side of the pin must hold against the flat side of the axle. Some axles will have a notch; others four flat sides. Have the notch or a flat side pointing straight back. Point the crank backward. Insert the pin with the threads down and the flat side forward. Place a block over the pin and use a few sharp hammer blows. Tap the cotter pin in place. At least ¼ inch of threads must stick out below. If not, remove the pin, and lightly file the flat side until you can get the desired thread exposure. Now you can install the washer and nut. The chainwheel side goes on the same way. Be sure the cranks are pointed in opposite directions—or prepare for some laughs on your first ride.

The cotterless cranks slip back on the four-sided axle. Get it lined up so you don't have to force it back on. If the square hole gets botched, it probably never will be on tight. If you put light oil on the axle end and in the square hole, it'll go on easier. Once it's completely seated, insert the bolt with washer into the axle hole and turn it by hand as far as you can. Then turn it down tight with the crank socket. Replace the dust cap.

Before you head down the road, you'll have to replace the chain (Chapter 14) and the pedals (as discussed earlier in this chapter).

Chainwheels—Front Sprockets

The front sprocket is the next step in transmitting your pedal power into rolling. On 1-speed, 3-speed, and 5-speed bikes, there is a single sprocket; on 10-speeds, two sprockets; and on 15-speeds, three sprockets.

About all you have to do to front sprockets is keep them clean and lightly oiled to prevent any rust. Generally, the proper lube care for your chain will keep the chainwheel oiled. The most common problems with a chainwheel are either a bent tooth or a wobbly sprocket.

Anybody with a toothache is going to tell you about it—your bike is no different. If you hear a funny *thunk* each time your pedaling cycle reaches a certain point, it's probably your bike calling your attention to a bent tooth. Get the back wheel off the ground and slowly turn the crank. A bent tooth will cause the chain to hump up each time the bad tooth comes around. Once you've found the tooth, mark it with a grease pencil and remove the chain. Make sure it's not cracked or broken—these teeth can't be capped. If it's merely bent, you can straighten it. A small bend can often be corrected without removing the chainwheel. If you can grip the bent tooth with a pair of lock grip pliers or an adjustable wrench and have room to move in the right direction, don't remove the assembly. On a two-sprocket chainwheel, this may not be possible. Grip above the point of the bend and apply slow, steady pressure. All you want to do is straighten one tooth, not bend the whole thing. Check as soon as you think it bent back at all. You'll break off a tooth if you have to work it back and forth.

If you can't make any headway (and some alloys are tough to bend), take off the sprocket and sandwich it between two boards. Put it on a solid surface and straighten with hammer blows. Use hardwood, or the bent tooth will just dig into the wood.

A wobbly sprocket may be bent, or the crank arm may not be properly attached. Check all the bolts. If it still wobbles, you'll have to apply the sandwich technique. If it's a one-piece crank and chainwheel, you'll only be able to sandwich the bent part. In that case, be careful to see that you isolate the bend and determine its direction. A close look may show that it's not a bent chainwheel, but a bent crank. Go back to cranks.

If you have to change a chainwheel, it's not a mean task. A one-piece crank for a 1-speed, and many 3-speeds, will all be one unit, so you'll have to get an entire assembly.

If the chainwheel is removable from the crank, remove the chain and take the right crank off the bottom bracket axle. The nuts and bolts that connect the two are easily removed. If there is more than one sprocket, don't lose the spacers in between.

In buying a new chainwheel, you have to make sure the holes where the crank will be attached are the same. You can drill new holes if there is metal to drill through at the right places. The bike shop will usually have one that's right. Take either the old chainwheel or a tracing to get the right one. The new sprocket can have a different number of teeth. This does change the gear ratio. More teeth mean a higher gear, and fewer teeth a lower gear. A change in teeth count could be incompatible with the chain you have, but probably not. Check it though. You may have to add links. The bike shop cycle-analyst will have specs on this.

The only thing to watch in installation is to tighten the bolts down a little at a time, moving from one to another. Turning one down all at once can pull something out of line—probably your new chainwheel.

When you get it all back together, be sure to check for proper chain tension (Chapter 14).

Freewheels—Rear Sprockets

The rear sprocket on a 1-speed bike, and on geared bikes with multispeed hubs, will have a single small sprocket. About all that can happen to it is the bent-tooth problem. The same possibilities for straightening exist here as previously discussed.

To remove the rear sprocket from a 1-speed, determine whether it's the type in Figure 70 that is held on by a threaded lock ring or the type in Figure 71 with a snap ring. With either one, you'll wish to remove the rear wheel (Chapter 10).

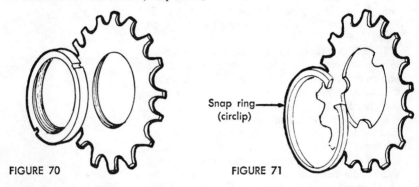

Snap ring—
(circlip)

FIGURE 70   FIGURE 71

13H-1. You'll also need to secure the other side of the hub, and a vise is the best method. Remember that metal vise jaws can chew into metal, so use a jaw softener—a piece of towel or rag between the vise and the hub.

13H-2. If it's a threaded sprocket, grab the tire with one hand and put a spanner wrench in the slots on the threaded lock ring. This comes off clockwise. If you don't have a spanner, get a friend to hold the tire while you tap a screwdriver angled into a slot.

13H-3. With the ring off, the sprocket comes off counterclockwise. There are tools designed for sprocket removal, such as the one shown here (Figure 72). If you don't have one and don't want one, the best way to loosen the sprocket is to put a few drops of penetrating oil around the threads. Try to remove it with your hands—your fingers will fit between the teeth for a pretty good grip. If that doesn't work, wrap an old towel around the

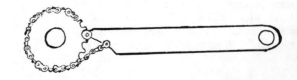

FIGURE 72

sprocket. Twist the towel until it's really tight, and using the twist part as a handle, you'll probably get it loose.

The snap ring holder comes off by prying the ring out of its groove with a screwdriver. The sprocket will lift straight off.

Before removing either kind, note which side of the sprocket faces out. Some have a shoulder outside, and others have one facing in. It has to go back the same way to line up.

13H-4. If yours has any spacers or washers, be sure to remember the order for proper reassembly.

While you've got it off, check the dust cap if there is one, and check the other parts shown to see if there's any damage.

There's no trick to reassembly.

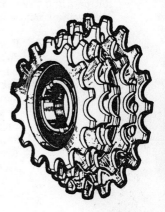

If your bike has a multispeed hub, you'll see how to get to the rear sprocket when we take the hub apart in Procedure 15A.

Now for freewheels—those clusters of sprockets in bikes with derailleur gears. These five different-sized sprockets come off easily, but you have to have a freewheel remover tool. Don't worry—the basic remover is quite inexpensive. There are two basic types—the splined and the pegged. A quick look at the outside end of the cluster will tell you which you need. If there are a series of V-shaped ridges around the axle, you need type A. If there are a pair of slots, get type B.

FIGURE 73

A

B

FIGURE 74

Freewheel Removers

109

13I-1. To remove the freewheel, the back wheel has to be off. (Refer to 10F.)

13I-2. Completely remove the axle nuts and whatever washers. If you have quick-release hubs, take these and the springs off.

13I-3. Next, remove the locknut, washers, and spacers. Keep track of the sequence, as it varies.

13I-4. If you have a splined assembly, insert the tool into the notches. Be sure the splines are well engaged in the ridges. Screw the axle nut back on down against the tool so it has to stay in place. (On quick-release jobs, the conical adjusting nut should be used.)

A slotted assembly uses the pegged tool. Engage the pegs in the slots and put the axle nut or conical quick-release nut on good and tight for this type.

13I-5. First, set an adjustable wrench on the end of the tool. Splined tools have square ends, and pegged have six-sided. Straddle the wheel and give the wrench a quick jerk in a counterclockwise direction. If it doesn't come loose after a few jerks, you may have to clamp the tool in a vise and turn the wheel to loosen. Rotate the wheel counterclockwise to loosen.

13I-6. Soon as it breaks loose (you hope that's what broke), remove the axle nut and tool and spin the entire unit off.

13I-7. To overhaul and check all the cluster parts, you must dismantle it. Many units will have a flat screw-on ring called a chain protector. It will probably screw off with a spanner wrench. (Use penetrating oil for the toughies.) It and the first three smaller sprockets come off counterclockwise.

13I-8. On some units, the third, fourth, and fifth sprockets are not threaded as in Figure 75. They are lugged and fit into notches on the cluster body. They lift right off. If all sprockets are threaded, the two largest ones are turned clockwise to remove (Figure 76).

Between each two sprockets are spacers. The units with all-threaded sprockets will have wide-threaded lips that space them from the next piece. The lugged units have separate spacer rings.

Put all the parts in solvent and brush them clean. Remove the cluster body and check to see if any threads are damaged. If it has splines, check them over. Turn the outside part clockwise to see that it

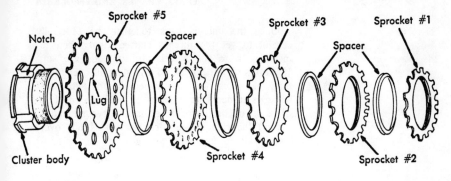

Notch

Sprocket #5

Spacer

Sprocket #3

Sprocket #1

Lug

Spacer

Cluster body

Sprocket #4

Sprocket #2

FIGURE 75

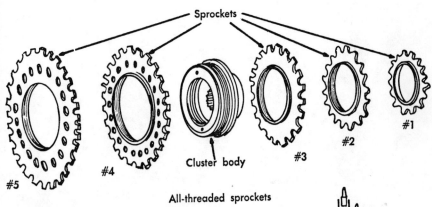

Sprockets

Cluster body

#5

#4

#3

#2

#1

All-threaded sprockets

FIGURE 76

wheels freely. Turn it counterclockwise to see that a clicking noise is made. Examine all sprocket teeth for bends, breaks, or rough spots. To straighten bends, try the same tactics discussed on pages 106 and 107 for chainwheels. Rough spots can possibly be removed with a fine-toothed file. Check threads and/or lugs. Be sure the spacers, if any, aren't bent.

Replace any bad parts, lightly oil, and with everything shipshape, reverse the process to put it all back together. The only caution in reassembly is to be sure the spacing is equal (Figure 77). Also, remember that the all-threaded clusters have two sprockets with left-hand threads.

All five sprockets
same distance apart

FIGURE 77

111

Once the unit is back together, be especially careful to get the threads started right when re-installing it to the wheel. Hub threads are soft. If it turns on hard, back off and start all over rather than take a chance on stripped threads. The free-wheel is turned clockwise to go back on the hub. Light oil on the hub threads is also recommended.

Find the right place for whatever is left over, hook it all up, and away you go.

14

Chains

The best way to check your chain is with it completely off the bike. This is easy to do, but you need to take it apart. If you have a non-derailleur-equipped bike, it's best to loosen the rear axle nuts so you can slide the wheel slightly forward. This slackens the chain and makes it easier to work with.

There are basically two types of bike chains: those with removable or connector links and those without. The former are generally found on bikes without derailleurs, and the latter on those with. The type with the removable job is quite easy to disconnect. The only problem is to track down the connecting link. It will look a tiny bit different, but not so much that you can pick it out at a glance. Usually, it requires a link-by-link inspection tour. It's often the next to last link you inspect—so instead of starting around the way you intended, inspect backward. Or better still, once you've found it, put a tiny drop of enamel paint on the connector link and you'll never have to inspect again. Whether the connector is a snap-on or spring-held (Figure 78), it's a snap to remove. The snap-on type snaps off with the flick of a screwdriver and a tiny bit of flexing of the chain. The spring-held type requires only that the open end of the spring plate be pried up, moved around (per the arrow in Figure 78), and lifted off. This reveals the plate which is lifted right off.

The other type of bike chain requires an inex-

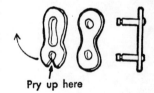

Pry up here

Split link spring

Snap-on link

FIGURE 78

pensive tool called a rivet extractor. The super drawing (Figure 79) shows this tool in place. To put it into action, all you have to do is turn the handle clockwise. Turn until the rivet is out. Turn the extractor back out, and the chain comes apart. This same tool is used to replace the rivet when you want to reconnect. Just place the rivet against the hole, and turn the tool until the tip touches the rivet. Line up the rivet, and then turn clockwise until the rivet is pressed back into its original position.

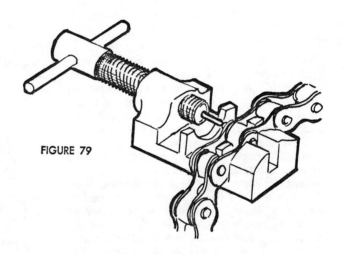

FIGURE 79

Lube your chain

Many times, the extra energy your bike is requiring from you to get moving is due to the lack of lubrication on your chain. As you can see from the diagram, the rollers are free to turn, and if they are dry, the turning requires more effort from *you!* If you want to do it right, you'll have to remove the chain. Whether you can see much grime or not, your chain is probably dirty, so while it's coiled up there like a snake, put it in a container of solvent, go in and steal a vegetable brush from the kitchen, and soak and scrub.

Now that it's clean—it's clean, isn't it?—let it dry, then dip it in a container of lightweight motor oil. Hang it up and let the excess drip back into the container. (If you buy a quart can of motor oil for this purpose, use a regular can opener and remove the entire lid. Recap with a plastic coffee can lid— the pound size exactly fits and will seal the can. Mark the can for chain lube, and you'll be able to use it over and over for a long time.) When the chain has quit dripping, put it back on.

Let's face it, not one in 307 readers will remove the chain just to lubricate it. So, for you lazies, clean it by dipping a rag in solvent. Move the chain through the soaked rag so solvent gets on all parts. Some of it will get under the rollers, and you'll get it fairly clean. Then take a rag and soak it in light-weight oil. Move the chain through the rag several times so a light coat of oil is all over the chain.

> RULE OF THUMB: *Too much oil on your chain holds grit and is just about as bad as no oil at "oil"—but not quite.*

Every so often, take an oiler can and put a drop on each roller as you turn the chain through a complete revolution. This will insure oil under the rollers.

Anytime you do have the chain off, give it a link-by-link inspection. If there's no evidence of damage, check it to see if it's stretched. (Chains do stretch!) Wrap the chain around the largest chain-wheel as shown in Figure 80. Then grab it at the arrow at the top and pull straight up. If it can be pulled up off the sprocket, it's stretched and is going to need to be replaced.

FIGURE 80

Chain Tension

After the chain is back in place, or even if you didn't take it off, the tension should be checked. Proper tension is critical. A too-tight chain forces you to exert extra effort and creates extra wear on the bike. A too-loose (not Lautrec) chain will skip.

The key is to use only as much tension as needed. Here's how to set and check it.

For a 1-speed bike, and for bikes with gears in the hub, the tension is set by loosening the mounting nuts on the rear axle and moving the wheel backward or forward to adjust the chain tension. Place a yardstick from front to rear sprocket. Look at the halfway point between sprockets. When there is ½-inch sag from the bottom of the yardstick to the bottom of the chain, tighten the nuts back. (Make sure the wheel is aligned. See 10F.)

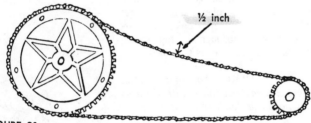

½ inch

FIGURE 81

FIGURE 82

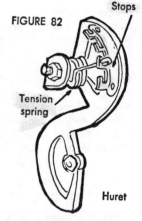

Stops

Tension spring

Huret

Derailleur-equipped bikes vary by makes as to the tension adjustment. The rear derailleur adjusts the tension as it moves. It automatically takes up slack, since a different length of chain is required for the different-size sprockets. If, when the chain is on the smallest sprockets both front and rear, the derailleur can't take up all the slack, the chain is too loose. When on the largest sprockets, there should be about ½-inch sag or it's too tight. Normally, you won't have too tight a chain with derailleurs if it was the right length to begin with.

Here are ways to adjust tension on most models:

14A-1. Huret Allvit (same as one of Schwinn Approved) has a tension spring (Figure 82). Move it to a higher stop to increase chain tension, and a lower one to decrease. Huret Svelto and Luxe models also have springs and stops.

14A-2. Simplex (applies to both Prestige and Criterium—(Figure 83)) has a slot for a hex wrench in the bolt at the bottom of the outer arm. It may also have a dust cap to be removed. Loosen the locknut located between the body and the cage. Using the proper hex wrench, turn the bolt clockwise to tighten, and counterclockwise to loosen.

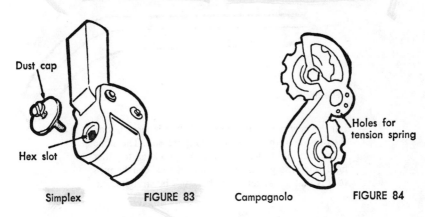

Dust cap

Hex slot

Simplex   **FIGURE 83**

Holes for tension spring

Campagnolo   **FIGURE 84**

14A-3. Campagnolo and Benelux (Figure 84) have a tension spring enclosed in a cover. With the chain off the derailleur, undo the small stop bolt. This will allow the cage—the part with the rollers—to unwind. Loosen the pivot bolt that runs through the spring cover and attaches to the derailleur cage. The outer cage plate will have holes in which the tip of the spring fits. Note which hole. Move it to the next hole counterclockwise to remove slack (turn the cage plate clockwise). Turn vice versa to loosen. Tighten the pivot bolt back. To rewind the spring, turn the cage one complete turn counterclockwise and fix it there with the stop bolt. If, when you shift to the big sprockets, the chain is too tight, undo the stop bolt and move the cage another half-turn counterclockwise.

14A-4. Shimano Lark has much the same chain tension adjustment. However, when you remove the chain cage stop bolt, you should hold the cage. With the stop bolt out of the way, wind the cage one turn clockwise to increase tension, or a turn counterclockwise to decrease it.

14A-5. Sun Tour is adjusted the same as the Lark above even though it looks quite different.

Chainguards

Time was when all decent self-respecting bikes had chainguards of the type shown in Figure 85. They still make 'em, and lots of bikes come with them,

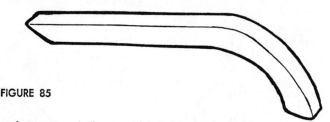

FIGURE 85

but the new type is the round job that is mounted on the outside of the chainwheel (Figure 86). The same bolts that hold the chainwheel sprockets together hold this type guard on. About all that can happen to it is that it can get bent. If it can't be straightened,

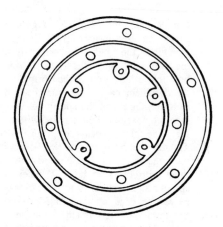

FIGURE 86

it's easy to replace. My only tip is that you shift so the chain is on the outside sprocket. As you remove the fastening bolts on the outside, reinsert them from the back to keep the spacers from getting lost. This also aids you in keeping the sprockets together. You'll

118

be able to replace without having to take anything else apart. Be sure the new one has holes that match up with the bolts. Also, if there are washers or spacers, keep them in tow—or a tin can if there's not a tow around.

The old-type guards are usually held by very obvious clamps that grab the frame. They have equally obvious nuts and bolts and not so obvious washers. These guards have a habit of moving ever so slightly, so either the chain or the crank hits on them. All you can do to take care of this is check the bolts every so often to be sure the brackets don't get loose, or bend the guard back away from what it's hitting.

Something caught in the chain?

Hopefully, if something gets caught in the chain, it's your pants and not a toe. The best way to get whatever it is uncaught is to crank the pedals backward. (With a coaster-brake bike, walk the bike backward.) Next time wear shorts or a pants clip, or be more careful.

Here's a pants-clip idea sent in by a reader who calls himself the "Old Pedaler":

"With the resurgence of bicycling as a pastime, and with the popularity of flared pants, maybe an old trick I used as a kid will keep some of those flares from getting caught in the chain. Rather than pay for pants clips, I made mine from 1-inch wide strips of an old inner tube. The strips should be just long enough to reach around the ankle. On one end of the strip, I cut a point like an arrowhead. The strip was tapered back from the arrowhead. The narrow point where the taper starts is about a quarter-inch. At the other end, I punched two holes a half-inch apart and made a slit between them. The slit runs lengthwise. When this is stretched around the pants leg, the point of the strip is poked into the slit and will hold the pants tight against the ankle. I would make several of these at a time and loop them around the bike seat post so I'd always have a spare if one got lost or broken."

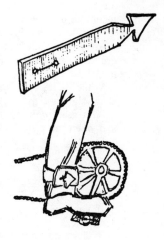

FIGURE 87

15

Gears

_____ **A shifty situation**

The two basic types of gears are the hub (or internal) gears and the derailleur (or external) gears. Hub gears are located inside the rear hub and can come in 2-, 3-, 4-, and 5-speed. Most 3-speed bikes have hub gears. A little later on, we'll tell you about a conversion kit for certain 3-speeds that will make them into 6- or 9-speeds.

Derailleur gears involve delicate mechanisms, but when properly adjusted they are really a joy for the cyclist. These can include the 5-, 10-, or 15-speed models.

While we're at it, here are a few rules of thumb about shifting derailleurs—_very important!_

Shift gears _only_ when the back wheel is moving and when the pedals are moving forward.

Don't strain against the pedals when shifting. Ease up a little, but don't stop pedaling.

Never back-pedal when shifting.

Shift only one or two steps at a time.

Do not force the shifting lever.

If your bike has two levers, shift only one lever at a time.

Maybe you have gears on your bike and really don't know what they are supposed to do. Lots of folks just shift when the going gets tough. If it seems easier to pedal after they shift, they leave it alone. If it makes the going tougher, they shift around until they find easier going or until they get back to where they were in the first place. No matter what system your bike has, *low* means the same thing. All you have to do is figure out when to use *low* and *high,* and how to shift into these, and you've got it made. Then you can start finding out what all the gears in between will do. Here is an old adage that I just made up that will explain when to use what. *"Low* when it's hard to go . . . *high* when it's easy to fly."* If you come to a hill, shift into low gear. When you get to the top and start to go down, shift into high, and for normal level pedaling, use medium.

Using that simple *high, low, medium* example explains all you need to know about 3-speeds. Except that some levers are marked 1, 2, and 3. Since 1 is the lowest number, you can figure that one. Sometimes there'll be *L, N,* and *H.* The *low* and the *high* are easy, but the *normal* is confusing because sometimes there's a *neutral.*

But what about 10-speeds? It's just expanded, so you have lower lows and higher highs. With a freewheel in the back, you have five different-sized sprockets, and thus, five gears. The smallest is the highest, and the largest is the lowest. The right lever selects the rear sprocket. Full forward on most systems shifts to the smallest sprocket, and all the way back takes it to the largest. The chainwheel on a 10-speed has two front sprockets so that when you're on one front sprocket, you have the five gears, and with the other front sprocket, you have five additional gears. The left lever moves the chain from one front sprocket to the other. Forward puts it on the small one, and back moves it to the large one. On front sprockets, the size thing is opposite in that the larger sprocket is high and the smaller low. So the highest high gear would be with the chain on the big front sprocket, and the least back one. (Left lever back and right lever full forward.)

By moving the right lever back in the 5 position, you shift down.

With both levers forward, you're right in the middle range. The lowest gear on a 10-speed is with the chain on the front smaller sprocket and the largest rear sprocket. (Left lever forward and right lever full back.)

The best way to learn about the different gears is through riding and trying. Before long you'll know what shifting to do under what conditions. You can change the gear ratio on your bike by installing different sprockets. Get your cycle-analyst to give you a gear ratio chart to see just what a few more teeth will do.

Hubs With Multispeed Gears

Bikes with 3-speeds, 4-speeds, 2-speeds, and some 5-speeds have gears inside the rear hub. While the range is not as wide as the 10-speed (Gosh, it took a lot of smarts to figure that out!), multispeed hubs are much more reliable than derailleur gears. Keep 'em oiled, cleaned, and occasionally adjusted and forget 'em. It's indeed fortunate that these babies are so reliable because there are those who will take one look at the many complicated parts inside and throw up their hands—others will just throw up. There are also multispeed hub makers who say, "Don't take it apart. If anything goes wrong, take it to an authorized repair shop." I'll let you decide for yourself. I do recommend that you get an exploded view of your rear hub—er, your bike's rear hub. The ones I have included will cover many, but not all. If you can't get the manufacturer to send this, and you still want to tear into the thing, make your own drawing as you go. If you're mechanically inclined and have lots of time on your hands, you can do it!

Meanwhile, let's consider adjusting and oiling so we won't have to overhaul. Most of the hubs will have a flip-top oiler cap on the shell of the hub. Use this every month. Squirt in light motor oil (30w) and run it through all the gears. Repeat the squirt and run again. Make sure the snap cap is back in place. Roll the bike so this cap faces down to make sure no oil is going to leak out.

Gear adjustment is quite simple. Figure 88 is typical of the setup whereby the cable and indicator chain enter a 3-speed hub. These adjustments apply to Sturmey-Archer units with the designations AW, AB, AG, TCW, and TCW Mark III, as well as several ripoffs by other companies. Shift into the

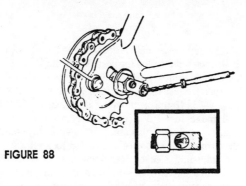

FIGURE 88

middle gear. This may be *N* for *normal* or 2 or *medium,* or just a blip or two in the middle of the shifter lever or twist grip. Now go back to the chain guide and look into the little hole. The end of the indicator rod should be exactly even with the end of the axle. If not, unscrew the locknut just below the adjusting sleeve. Twist the adjuster sleeve until the rod lines up. Reposition the locknut, and the adjustment for all three gears is made. Easy? You bet.

If there's not enough or too much cable to allow for this adjustment, there is a fulcrum clip that holds the cable to the frame. Loosen this and adjust the fulcrum sleeve back or forth to move the cable as needed.

The types of Sturmey-Archer designated as FW, FM, FG, SW, AM, ASC, and AC (as well as the copies) are adjusted the same way as above. However, the indicator check is made on the left side of the bike. The middle gear will position the end of the indicator rod even with the left end of the axle (Figure 89).

If you have a 3-speed Shimano 333, there'll be a bell crank unit (Figure 90). It has a letter *N* that appears in the center of a cut-out circle when the lever is in the middle gear. To line it up, loosen the locknut and turn the sleeve. When it's lined up, tighten the locknut.

The Sturmey-Archer S5 is a 5-speed multihub job. It has dual control levers and cables that enter both sides of the hub. The right side is adjusted just as with the first group, with the indicator rod lining up with the axle on the right side while the right lever is in the center and the left lever full forward.

FIGURE 89

Left end
indicator rod
lineup

FIGURE 90

Shimano 333 Bell Crank

123

The left lever cable doesn't need any adjusting if it passes the following test. With the lever all the way back, gently push the bell crank arm in Figure 91 forward. At the same time, rotate the rear wheel backward. If the gear isn't fully engaged, the arm will move forward a little more. That means you need to tighten the cable more—possibly pushing the arm more. Loosen the knurled locknut and turn the adjusting sleeve. Retighten the locknut. Since there are but two positions on the left lever, once you are sure it's in gear when the lever is back, you should be all set.

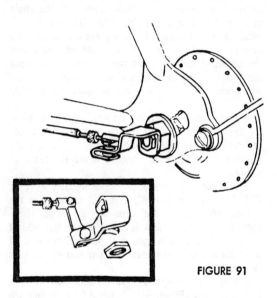

FIGURE 91

Meanwhile, back at the hub: you've adjusted and lubed and fiddled, and it still doesn't work. You've decided the trouble is inside the hub—furthermore, you've decided that if the kid next door can tear down and rebuild his hot rod, you can certainly overhaul your hub.

124

Sturmey-Archer AW • This British-made system is probably on more of the 3-speed bikes around than any other. The key to this gear working is shown in the drawing in Figure 92. The cogged wheel in the center is called the sun gear or sun wheel—the ones around it are planet gears. The sun wheel is attached to the axle so it's fixed. The planets have pins on which they rotate. Planet gear teeth are meshed with sun gear teeth and with the gear ring.

FIGURE 92

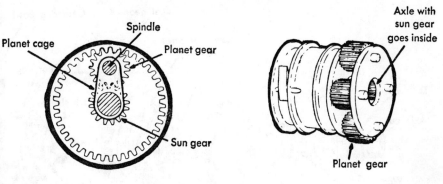

Planet cage

Spindle

Planet gear

Sun gear

Axle with
sun gear
goes inside

Planet gear

By changing the driving force from planet gears to gear ring, the ratio of speed of the turning parts inside to the sprocket outside changes. In *high,* the hub is driven faster than the sprocket; in *low,* it rotates slower. In *normal,* the force doesn't go through the gears, and the wheel and sprocket travel as a unit at the same speed.

Just because you don't understand anything about how it works doesn't mean you can't take it apart and put it back together. Let's give it a go. Lay out a large towel—not the guest towel. Even though the sequence shown in Figure 93 is from a service manual, yours may be different. So as you take parts off, lay them out in order across the towel. Put the bike in high gear, undo the cable at the rear wheel, and remove the wheel. (See 10-F.) This thing has so many parts that in order to do the right thing to the right part, you should refer to Figure 94 before each step.

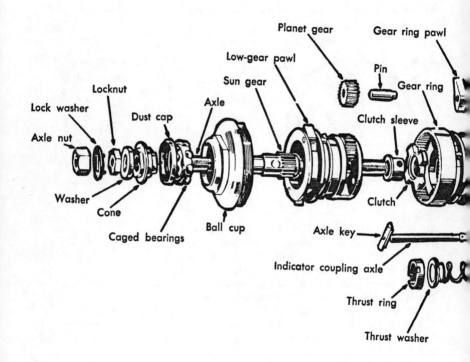

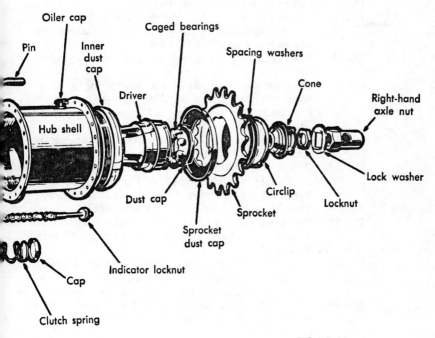

Oiler cap

Pin

Inner dust cap

Caged bearings

Spacing washers

Cone

Right-hand axle nut

Driver

Hub shell

Dust cap

Sprocket dust cap

Sprocket

Circlip

Locknut

Lock washer

Indicator locknut

Cap

Clutch spring

FIGURE 93

15A-1. Undo the left-hand cone locknut along with washers.

15A-2. Unscrew the left-hand cone.

15A-3. Check the notches on the right-hand ball ring. One notch will have the letters *SA* stamped on it. Put a piece of masking tape on the spoke nearest this notch.

15A-4. Now remove the ball ring. You'll probably have to place a screwdriver in a notch and tap to break the ring loose. Although it's unscrewed, it won't come off.

15A-5. Now the entire unit can be pulled straight out of the hub.

15A-6. Make sure no parts are left inside.

15A-7. Put the unit in a vise with the right side sticking up. Be sure to avoid chewing up the left-end threads on the axle as you clamp it in the vise!

15A-8. There is a spring clip against the outside of the sprocket. Pry it up.

15A-9. There are washers—usually two—next to the sprocket. Sometimes they are on one side only—sometimes on both sides. They have to go back exactly as they came off, so make note of the order.

15A-10. Also, note the inset on the sprocket, and whether it faces in or out. These parts lift off.

15A-11. Next remove the pins that hold the low-gear pawls. They are held by tiny clip springs, and once the spring is flipped off, they slide straight out. Don't lose the pawls. Don't lose the springs. Don't lose your cool.

15A-12. Now you'll want to remove the locknut and cone from the right side. Here again there are washers to keep track of.

15A-13. With these gone, you can now lift off the clutch spring and its cap, the driver, the right-hand ball ring, and the gear ring. Do you wish you'd never started this project?

15A-14. Incidentally, inside the right-hand ball ring there is a pressed-in dust cover with ball bearings. Don't try to remove them.

15A-15. The next step is to remove the other pawls on the gear ring, along with their pins and springs.

15A-16. See the thrust ring? Take it out and unscrew the indicator rod.

15A-17. Push the axle key out. Then remove the sliding clutch and the clutch sleeve.

15A-18. The planet cage should next be lifted off. By removing the pins, planet gears come out.

15A-19. Next, remove the left-hand ball cup by turning clockwise.

You should now have parts spread from one end of the towel to the other. On this first go-around, clean and inspect the parts individually instead of dumping the entire lot in the solvent.

Check all parts for wear or breakage.

See that the sliding clutch slides freely in the driver.

Examine the axle to be sure it's straight and without wear or scratches.

Look over all bearings for wear or pitting. Check to be sure the cages aren't bent.

Make sure the races aren't worn or pitted.

Inspect the teeth on the sun gear, planet gears, and gear ring for wear or chipped places. Also, check for these problems with the pawls and ratchets.

Be certain there are no botched threads.

Well, now, that wasn't so bad, was it? Take any bad parts along to make sure you get exact replacements. Don't be discouraged when the bike shop guy says, "Lotsa luck on getting it back together."

To assemble the whole mess, you pretty much reverse the process, but with some exceptions. Let's go through it step by step.

15B-1. Put a coat of light grease in the channels of the dust cap that snaps into the left-hand ball cup.

15B-2. Don't forget this ball cup has to be turned counterclockwise to replace it. (Or, since it's a British-made part, maybe we should say, "anti-clockwise.")

15B-3. While you have the grease out, smear some in the race in the driver and in the recess of the right-hand ball ring, and then put the grease away because you won't use it again.

15B-4. Place the gear ring unit down flat with the teeth side down. You're going to replace its pawls. Be sure you didn't get pawls mixed up since gear-ring pawls are different from low-gear pawls. Center the spring loop over the pawl pin hole. Grip the long nose of the pawl and the foot of the spring with your thumb and forefinger, making sure the spring loop stays centered over the hole. Slide the pawl back in place in the gear ring tail first. When the pawl hole is lined up with the flange hole, push the pin in place.

15B-5. Put the left end of the axle back down in the vise with

129

all but about an inch sticking up. (Right end up.)

15B-6. Slip the planet cage in place against the sun gear.

15B-7. Replace the planet gears and fix them with the pins. Remember, the small end is the part that sticks out.

15B-8. Now slip the clutch sleeve down over the axle—the flange side goes down. Line up the hole in the sleeve with the slot in the axle.

15B-9. Slip the sliding clutch over so its recess fits over the sleeve and down around the flange.

15B-10. Slip the axle key in through the hole in the sleeve, through the axle slot, and out the other side of the sleeve. Be sure the flat ends of the axle key face up.

15B-11. Insert the indicator rod into the axle and engage it in the axle key and screw it in place.

15B-12. Slide the thrust ring and its washer over the axle so its notches fit over the axle key.

15B-13. Pick up the gear ring assembly you prepared earlier and fit it down over the planet cage. Make sure its teeth slip over the teeth of the planet gears.

15B-14. Fit the right-hand ball cup down against the gear ring assembly. (Be sure it still has the pressed-in dust cap with fixed bearings inside. You didn't remove them.)

15B-15. Put the caged bearings into the grease race in the driver unit with the balls facing in, and fit this in place.

15B-16. Follow this with the clutch spring and its cap, if separate.

15B-17. Place the right-hand cone on the axle and screw it down hand tight.

15B-18. Put the locknut on, but before it reaches the cone, back the cone up a half-turn *exactly*. Screw the locknut on down.

15B-19. Next, you replace the low-gear pawls. This is best done with the unit in a vise with the left end of the axle pointing up. Slip the pawls in place between the two flanges with the long side in and with the flat driving side pointing right. Line up the holes and push the pin about half way through the hole from the top flange. Using tweezers, pull the spring under the pawl until the loop lines up with the hole and both legs of the spring are between the pawl and the cage. Push the pin on through. If the job has been done right, the pawl will stay in the position with the driving edge up.

15B-20. While the unit is still in this position, I'd suggest you put about two teaspoons of 30w oil into the cage.

15B-21. Now pick up the wheel and slip the hub shell over the axle.

15B-22. Take it out of the vise, but keep it tilted so the oil doesn't run out.

15B-23. Fit the right ball ring against the shell and screw it into place.

15B-24. If the *SA* mark doesn't line up with the spoke you taped, unscrew it and rotate the ring a half-turn and then restart it. It has two start threads, so if the first start didn't line up, the second will.

15B-25. Screw the left-hand cone on and apply its locknut and washers—if any.

15B-26. Slip the outer dust cap in place over the driver, and then put the sprocket in the grooves—making sure the washers are back like they were. Position the spring clip, and you're ready to replace the wheel in the drop outs and adjust the gears.

You deserve a hand and a tall cool one.

Next time, you'll be able to field strip the hub blindfolded.

TCW Mark III • This Sturmey-Archer unit is combined with a coaster brake as shown in the exploded view in Figure 94.

Undo the cable connection and remove the wheel. (See Procedure 10F.)

15C-1. With the sprocket end of the axle carefully clamped in a vise, remove the left locknut, the washer, and the brake arm nut.

15C-2. With these gone, you can remove the brake arm, the left cone dust cap, and the cone itself.

15C-3. Lift out the caged bearings and the brake band.

15C-4. Now remove the wheel from the vise and stand it upright. Read steps 15A-3 and 15A-4 for the removal of the right-hand ball ring.

15C-5. With the right-hand ball ring undone, lay the wheel on its left side and extract the entire unit—except for the planet cage pawl ring and the brake thrust plate. They're still in the shell and should be lifted out.

15C-6. Place the left end of the axle in the vise jaws—be careful of the threads. Undo the right locknut, the washers, and the right-hand cone. Make careful note of the sequence of these parts, as it varies.

15C-7. Now you can lift off the clutch spring, followed by the sprocket which is attached to the driver.

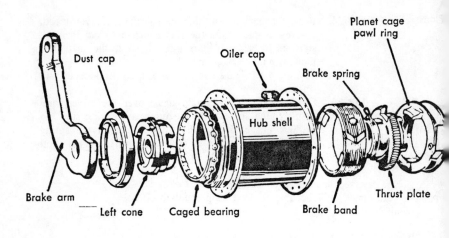

Dust cap

Oiler cap

Planet cage
pawl ring

Brake spring

Hub shell

Brake arm

Left cone

Caged bearing

Brake band

Thrust plate

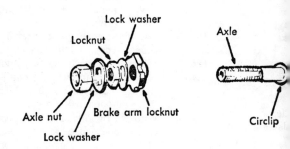

Lock washer

Locknut

Axle

Axle nut

Brake arm locknut

Lock washer

Circlip

TCW Mark III

Gear pin

Planet gear

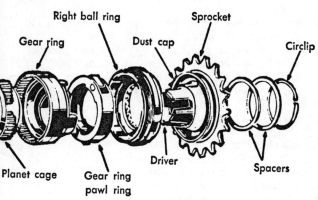

Right ball ring

Gear ring

Dust cap

Sprocket

Circlip

Planet cage

Gear ring
pawl ring

Driver

Spacers

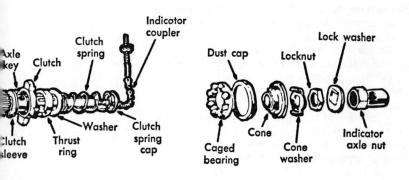

Axle
key

Clutch

Clutch
spring

Indicator
coupler

Clutch
sleeve

Thrust
ring

Washer

Clutch
spring
cap

Dust cap

Locknut

Lock washer

Caged
bearing

Cone

Cone
washer

Indicator
axle nut

FIGURE 94

15C-8. The previously loosened right-hand ball ring can now be lifted off.

15C-9. Next there's the gear ring pawl ring, and the gear ring itself.

15C-10. Lift off the thrust ring, along with its washer.

15C-11. Unscrew the indicator rod.

15C-12. This allows you to push the axle key out of the slot, and this releases the sliding clutch and sleeve.

15C-13. Next, remove the planet gears by pulling their pins out.

15C-14. Take the axle out of the vise and pry up the spring clip that's on the left end of the axle. This allows you to slip the planet cage off the end of the axle.

Now you've got parts spread out all over the towel.

Use the same clean-and-inspect routine following 15A-19.

In addition to the individual parts you have scattered around, there are several subassemblies, some of which you can further dismantle if need be.

The brake arm and the left-hand cone, along with its dust cap, are pressed into position. If you want to separate these parts, hold the brake arm in your left hand and tap lightly on the outer edge of the cone with a hammer. Then hold the cone dust cap between fingers of both hands, and with both of your thumbs, press the outer sides of the cone through the dust cap.

On the right-hand ball ring, there is a channel section dust cap, and this could be pried out with a screwdriver. The pawl pins cannot be removed from the gear ring or from the planet cage because they are riveted in place. If for some reason you decide that you have to have new pawls, and you want to do the job yourself, you are going to have to drill the pins out. Unless you happen to have the right kind of equipment, you won't be able to get them riveted back in place. This is one of those deals where you'll probably need to forget about replacing the small parts and replace the entire gear ring or planet cage.

Right now you're probably thinking that there is no way to get all that stuff back into the small shell, but have faith. You'll do it. Here are the steps to take to get it all back together. It's best to put together several different subassemblies first, and then start putting these back in the proper place.

15D-1. Pick up the sprocket. It has the driver attached to it. Smear a little grease into the driver and put the caged bearings in place with the balls facing in.

15D-2. Take the left cone and the left dust cap and position them so that the slots in the dust cap register with the slots in the cone.

15D-3. Next, press the brake arm tightly into the slots in the left-hand cone. Be sure you've got the brake arm on right. The brand name should be facing out to the left.

15D-4. Next, position the right end of the axle in the vise. Make sure that enough of the axle is sticking out so that the axle key slot is still accessible.

15D-5. Slip the planet cage over the axle with the planet gears on the bottom.

15D-6. Can you still find the little spring clip? If you can, slip it in place so that it holds the planet cage on the axle.

15D-7. Now take the axle out of the vise and put the left end back in the vise. Be careful of those threads.

15D-8. Slip the planet gears back in place. Put in the pins with the flattened ends headed down.

15D-9. Now slip the clutch sleeve on with the flange headed down and put the sliding clutch down over this. Make sure that it fits down over the flange in the sleeve. Line up the hole in the sleeve with the slot in the axle and slip the axle key in place with the flat ends of the key facing upward.

15D-10. Next, insert the indicator rod into the axle and screw it into the axle key to hold all these parts in their proper place.

15D-11. Now fit the thrust ring and its washer down over the axle. Make sure that the notches in the thrust ring fit down over the flat ends of the key and lock in place.

15D-12. Next comes the gear ring. Make sure that the heads of the pawl pins are facing upward.

15D-13. The right-hand ball ring assembly goes on next.

15D-14. This is followed by the previously prepared driver sprocket assembly.

15D-15. Next, drop the clutch spring over the axle.

15D-16. Place the right-hand cone on the axle and screw it down finger tight. Then back it up one half-turn—*exactly*.

15D-17. Place the locknut and whatever washers came off in place and lock the cone at this position.

15D-18. It's time to flip the assembly over again in the vise. At this time I would recommend that you put two teaspoonfuls of light motor oil (30w) down into the planet cage.

15D-19. Slip the planet cage pawl ring assembly in place.

15D-20. Find the brake thrust plate, and with the spring part facing upward, drop it in place on the axle, making sure that the slots in it fully engage in the dogs in the planet cage pawl ring.

15D-21. Now slip the brake band in place, making sure that the projections are facing upward.

15D-22. OK, it's time to take it out of the vise again and pick up the wheel. While holding the mechanism so it's still tilted upward so as not to spill the oil, and with the wheel facing downward, you can insert the unit back in its shell.

15D-23. To hold it there, screw the right-hand ball ring down tight. Remember that the *SA*-marked slot has to line up with the spoke that you put the tape over. If it doesn't, remove the ring and rotate it one half-turn and then engage the threads again. (This has what they call a two-start thread, so that if it doesn't line up the first go-around, it's got to line up the second time after rotation.)

15D-24. Now grease the race inside the left-hand ball cup lightly with light grease and drop the caged bearings with the balls down into place.

15D-25. Go back to the left-hand cone and brake arm assembly that you put together and make sure that the brake band projections and the spring on the thrust plate fit into their respective places in the cone.

15D-26. You are now ready to put the brake arm locknut and whatever washers came off with it in place.

Next, you are ready to replace the wheel into the drop outs, refasten the brake arm clips, and reconnect the chain and the cable.

Son-of-a-gun, you got it all back together! Take a ten-minute coffee break before you adjust as shown in Figure 88. After you've adjusted in the rack, take it for a ride, but be careful riding under a low bridge because your head will swell from having accomplished the feat of overhauling your TCW Mark III and getting it back together.

If you happen to have a TCW hub that is not a Mark III, you can follow almost the same procedure in dismantling and putting back together. However, the parts will look a little different. One thing to keep in mind is that almost none of the parts on the TCW old style are interchangeable with the Mark III.

While these very detailed instructions will cover a great percentage of the 3-speed hubs in the country, there are many, many other variations. In addition to half a dozen other Sturmey-Archer setups that are slightly different, a number of manufacturers have similar 3-speed hubs. If your hub is not covered, i would probably be a good idea to write to the manufacturer and ask for an exploded view, as well as the complete instructions on dismantling and reassembly. If it is from a foreign country, it will be worth a few laughs just trying to decipher the English translation of the instructions.

If you have a 5-speed multihub, chances are very good that it's going to be the Sturmey-Archer S5 shown in Figure 95.

To start with, follow exactly the same procedure described in the disassembly of the Sturmey-Archer AW hub. Go back and follow steps 15A-1 through 15A-10 until you get to the point where we remove the low-gear pawls. This is not going to be possible with the S5 because the pins are riveted in place.

15A-11A. Looking at the exploded view, you will find the dog ring. It's necessary to remove the locknut and washer so that you can remove this.
15A-12A. Now you can push the two sun gears on the axle and separate them to expose the second axle key.
15A-13A. This can be pushed out of place and will allow the two sun gears and the sleeve and spring to slide off the axle.

Unless there is some obvious flaw when you start checking everything out, don't take any of the other assemblies apart.

To clean and examine, go back to the section following 15A-19 and go through the checklist. In addition, with the S5 you have dogs on the axle to check for wear and dogs on the planet cage. If you have to replace any parts, be sure to take the bad

137

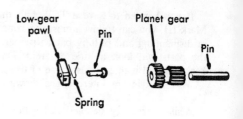

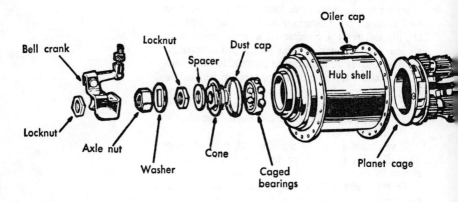

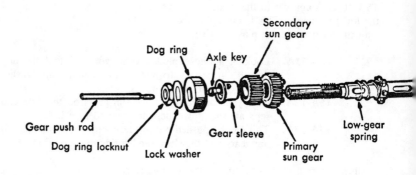

Sturmey-Archer 5-Speed Hub (S-5)

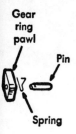

Gear
ring
pawl

Pin

Spring

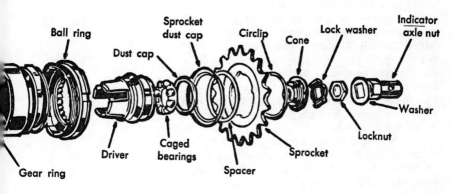

Ball ring

Dust cap

Sprocket
dust cap

Circlip

Cone

Lock washer

Indicator
axle nut

Washer

Locknut

Driver

Caged
bearings

Spacer

Sprocket

Gear ring

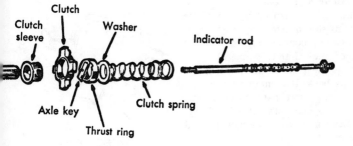

Clutch
sleeve

Clutch

Washer

Indicator rod

Axle key

Thrust ring

Clutch spring

FIGURE 95

guys along to make certain you get the exact same replacements. If everything is shipshape and clean and you have put light oil over all the parts after checking them, you are ready to put the thing back together again. Lots of luck.

Convert Your 3-Speed to a 6- or 9-Speed • If your 3-speed uses the Sturmey-Archer gears, and if you have decided you'd like the luxury of a wider range of gears, there is a conversion kit that you can get. It's a Cyclo Benelux kit available at many bike stores. The CB 70 is the 6-speed, and the CB 79 is the 9-speed. Complete instructions come with the kit, so there's no need for me to go into detail. However, before you buy the kit, you must know which type Sturmey-Archer your bike has. It will be either the AW or the SW. This designation will be stamped on the hub as shown.

Next, you have to determine if you have threads or splines. The drawings of each type will enable you to tell the difference. Chances are that if you bought your bike within the past eight years, it will be a splined driver.

You'll also have to add lengths to your chain—this is covered in Chapter 14.

Control Levers—Multispeed Hubs • The multispeed hub gears are usually changed by one of the three different systems shown here—the trigger type (Figure 96), the twist grip control (Figure 97), and the top-tube-mounted stick shift (Figure 99).

The trigger type is the pick of the three in my book—and this is my book. It's almost trouble free. The twist grip has a few more parts to go wrong. The stick shift is very popular with kids—it's flashy. If you have a 5-speed hub, we've already learned that you'll have two levers.

The trigger type requires only an occasional check to be sure the unit is still tightly attached to the handlebar, a drop of oil every month, and a kind word after a good ride. If, because you have done a dumb thing, you bend or break the unit, an entire new one costs only a couple of bucks.

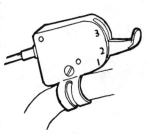

FIGURE 96

140

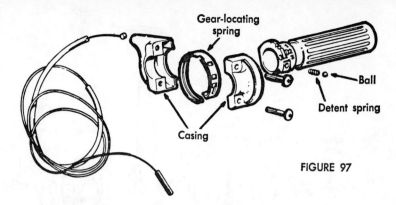

Gear-locating spring

Ball

Detent spring

Casing

FIGURE 97

The twist grip has more pieces—hence, more things to go wrong. To check it out, undo the two screws in the top half of the casing. Carefully remove the casing because there is a small steel bearing with a spring under it ready to spring out and roll down a drain. Capture both the spring and the ball. Now remove the top casing. Look at its backside, and you'll see the metal ring which is the gear-locating spring. Also, you'll see a slotted recess in the operating sleeve where the cable hooks. Lift the cable nipple out. Check the gear-locating spring to be sure it's not damaged, worn, or bent. Look at the race where the small ball travels from gear to gear to be sure it's smooth and even. See that the spring and ball are OK. Light grease on the ball and light oil on the moving parts will keep it twisting as it should.

There's another type of twist grip (Figure 98) that is called the "Old Style." It has a single bolt that holds its collar to the handlebar. The ball and detent spring fit in the collar.

FIGURE 98

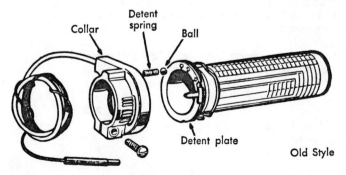

Collar

Detent spring

Ball

Detent plate

Old Style

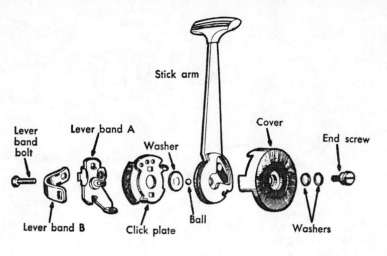

Stick arm

Lever band A

Lever
band
bolt

Washer

Cover

End screw

Lever band B

Click plate

Ball

Washers

FIGURE 99

The stick shift type we mentioned earlier may appeal to the youngsters, but it's not a Tinkertoy when it comes to overhaul. It is mounted on the top tube. Since most of these are blessed with plastic parts, they can self-destruct. If you're having trouble with one, remove the center screw which allows you to remove the plastic cover. Keep track of all the spacers, washers, and other small parts. Bathe the metal parts in solvent, and then check over all parts for wear, rust, cracks, and so forth. If you need replacements, you may have trouble finding parts. If so, talk your kid into graduating to a trigger shift. A few bucks will get a new unit and cable, and it's a snap to put on—it's almost trouble free! (Yes, you'll need a new cable, since the old one won't be long enough.)

Cables • The general care and keeping of cables for multispeed hubs is the same as for derailleur gears and will be taken up fully later in this chapter.

142

Derailleur Gears

The derailleur gears of your bike are responsible for more pleasure and more confusion, puzzlement, and agony than any other part. When working, they make riding a pleasure. When not, most people just throw up their hands. But derailleurs aren't that difficult.

Levers • The derailleurs are operated by cables that are moved by selector levers. Look at the exploded view of a 10-speed selector lever setup (Figure 100). Whether the levers are attached to the handlebar stem, the down tube, or the top tube, the same principles apply.

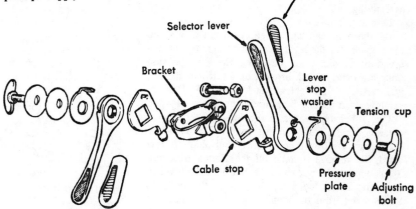

FIGURE 100

FIGURE 101

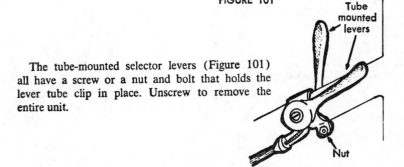

The tube-mounted selector levers (Figure 101) all have a screw or a nut and bolt that holds the lever tube clip in place. Unscrew to remove the entire unit.

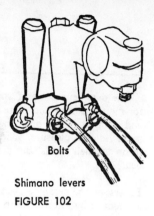

Shimano levers are held on by a pair of bolts on the front (Figure 102).

Huret Sprint levers are held on the stem by the locknut on the stem (Figure 103). The stem must be removed before you can get the levers off.

Another stem mount, the Sun Tour, requires stem removal also. It has a screw on the back of the clamp that holds it to the stem (Figure 104).

Once apart, they have much the same parts as in the exploded view. By holding the lever steady, the adjusting screw or bolt can be removed. When it's off, all the other parts can slide off. Since there are variances in the way these different parts look, it would be well to string them on a wire as they're removed to be sure of the right sequence when reassembling.

Disconnect the cable.

All the parts can be cleaned in solvent unless you have covers for the levers, or if the levers themselves are hard plastic. After cleaning, check to be sure none are bent, rusted, broken, or scratched. If bent, you can try to straighten, but lots of luck. Rust or scratches can usually be removed by fine steel wool.

One other type lever is the handlebar tip lever (Figure 105). This unit fits into the end of the handlebar. Its down position is equivalent to forward. To remove it, take off the slotted trim nut. Then remove the nut and bolt that hold the lever to the unit. When loosened, this allows the body to be removed from the handlebar. Clean all parts in solvent except lever covers. Make sure there are no bent, broken, scratched, or rusted parts. Bends can sometimes be straightened. Rust or scratches can sometimes be removed by fine steel wool.

Bolts

Shimano levers
FIGURE 102

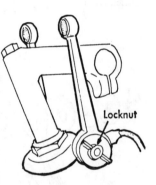

Locknut

Huret Sprint Levers
FIGURE 103

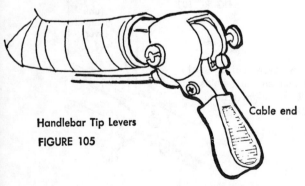

Handlebar Tip Levers
FIGURE 105

Cable end

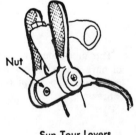

Nut

Sun Tour Levers
FIGURE 104

RULE of THUMB: Don't oil or grease the control lever parts. If they are smooth and work well, don't do anything. If they aren't, try WD-40 or silicone lube spray.

When together, adjustments are made by the wing screw. Tighten (clockwise) to firm up the movement, and unscrew to loosen. When properly adjusted, the levers should be a little stiff in moving, but not tight enough to be difficult.

The 5-speed derailleur gears will have only one lever that operates the rear assembly.

Cable • The next part of the gear arrangement is the cable. Usually, the cable and housings can be examined by eyeballing without taking anything apart. Check the cables for any frayed places. Also look for any spots where the cable has been flattened. Flattened or frayed cables should be replaced.

Inspect the housings for kinks or dents. Also, examine the ends for burrs. If you can file or snip the burr off, OK. Otherwise, cut off a tiny bit of the end to get a clean cut.

To cut housing, run a pocket knife around the plastic outer cover to expose the metal housing. Now, put the wire cutter blades against the housing and move them until they go in a ridge between coils. Once in the slot, start by applying light pressure. Rotate the cutter back and forth so the blades are cutting all around the housing. Keep rotating and gradually apply more pressure till you cut through. Be sure to check the new cuts for burrs too.

Also, test the tightness of cables. Figure 106 shows a typical anchor nut for a rear derailleur cable, and Figure 107 is for the front. Set the lever full forward. Grab the end of the cable with pliers and loosen the anchor nut. Pull the cable tight and anchor it back.

Cables also need lubrication—very light grease is best. This requires taking the cables off so the grease gets on the part of the cable inside the hous-

FIGURE 106
Typical Gear
Cable Anchors

Rear

FIGURE 107

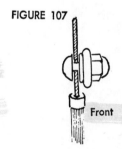

Front

145

ing. If the cable needs lubrication, and it's not in your horoscope to remove it today, squirt oil in at the housing ends and work the cable back and forth to distribute the oil.

If you're going to remove the cable, the chain should be on the smallest sprockets. For a 10-speed, this means the smallest chainwheel as well as the small rear sprocket. (The one exception: if you have a Sun Tour front derailleur unit, the chain should be on the large chainwheel.) Undo the cable anchor nuts. Now move the lever to the full rear position, and this should expose the cable end. Work it out of the slot in the lever and pull it out. (Sometimes the lever will have to be disassembled to get hold of the cable end.)

If you need a new cable, be sure the lever end is the same kind as the old one. You can see the difference in the two ends shown. There are others. Also, be sure to get a cable as long or longer than the old one. If it's longer, don't clip it off until it's installed and all derailleur adjustments are made.

Whether you are reinstalling an old or a new cable, grease it lightly all along. Insert it in the lever, and as you thread it through the lever and housings along its route, continually twist it in the opposite direction from the way it was wound in manufacturing it. This prevents the end of a strand from catching on anything as it goes through.

When the cable is all the way through the anchor nut, move the lever full forward. Grab the end of the cable with the pliers and pull it tight, and then anchor it there. With the back wheel turning, change gears a few times to be sure the cable lever and the derailleur are back together again.

Remember, a new cable can stretch, so check its tightness after a week or so.

The Rear Derailleur • Many people think that *derailleur* is a French word meaning "don't touch." They don't see how the little gadget does its thing, and so they figure all they'd do by touching it would be to throw it out of kilter. Don't shy away from your rear derailleur. In fact, a rear changer should be checked often for adjustment and alignment. It's a delicate mechanism, and if not kept up to snuff, it can self-destruct. No sense having to buy a new one when a few minor adjustments can keep it and you happy.

The rear changer moves the chain from one rear sprocket to another. At the same time, it adjusts the tension on the chain. It takes up the slack when not as much chain is needed for smaller sprockets.

Before you get to adjusting, look at the exploded super drawing (Figure 108) to see what the different parts are. Your derailleur may look different, but the same principle of operation holds true.

Let's check out and adjust your derailleur. The rear wheel should be off the ground, and:

RULE OF THUMB: *Never shift unless the pedals and the rear wheel are moving!*

15E-1. Check the mounting bolt to be sure the unit is on tight.

15E-2. Look to see if there's any obvious damage—a bent or broken part.

15E-3. Make sure the unit is clean, and if not, scrub it with solvent, and then lubricate.

15E-4. Check to be sure the middle sprocket of the freewheel cluster is lined up with the front sprocket on a 5-speed, or the center between the two front sprockets on a 10-speed. If not, this has to be corrected before you will ever get good rear changer adjustment. See Chapter 13 on chainwheels or freewheels, and Chapter 11 on frames.

15E-5. Turn the pedals and look to be sure the jockey wheel is tracking in the center of the chain. If not, this could be caused by either the mounting bracket or the derailleur cage being bent. Either one can be bent back in place, but *be gentle*. The best method is to use a pair of pliers and slowly straighten the guilty party. Usually, a slight twist is all you need.

15E-6. Now shift so the chain is on the largest front sprocket and the smallest rear sprocket. Inspect the cable—it should be almost tight, but not quite. If not, adjust as previously discussed.

15E-7. With the cable adjusted, turn the high-gear adjusting screw while turning the pedals until the derailleur cage is

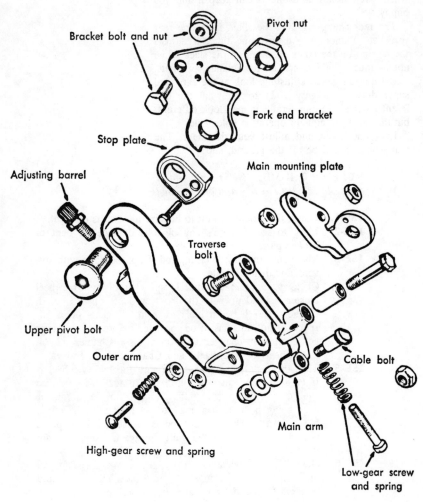

Bracket bolt and nut

Pivot nut

Fork end bracket

Stop plate

Main mounting plate

Adjusting barrel

Traverse bolt

Upper pivot bolt

Outer arm

Cable bolt

Main arm

High-gear screw and spring

Low-gear screw and spring

FIGURE 108

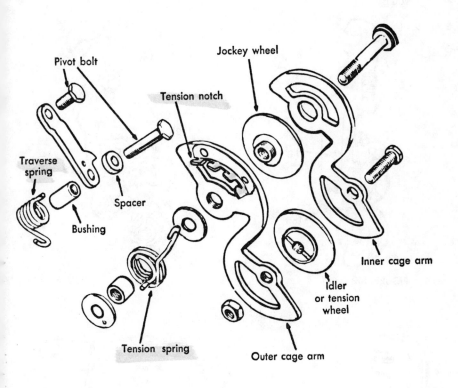

Pivot bolt

Jockey wheel

Tension notch

Traverse spring

Bushing

Spacer

Inner cage arm

Idler or tension wheel

Tension spring

Outer cage arm

exactly centered over the chain and the small sprocket. Figures 109, 110, and 111 show several different rear changers with the adjusting screws—both *high* and *low*—pointed out. Shift the lever so the chain moves off the small sprocket. Now shift it back again to the small one. Check to be sure the cage is again centered over the chain and the small sprocket. If not, do more adjusting until you get it right.

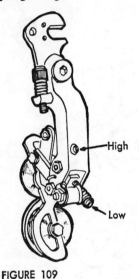

FIGURE 109

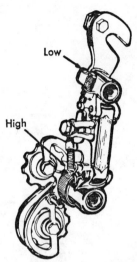

FIGURE 110

Adjusting rear derailleur

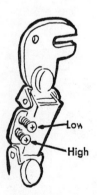

Lark (Shimano)

FIGURE 111

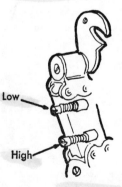

Simplex

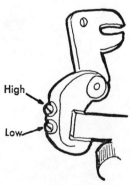

Sun Tour

15E-8. When you finally get it right (often the first time), shift so the chain goes over to the big rear sprocket. Now turn the low-gear adjusting screw until the guide cage is centered over the chain and the big sprocket. All set? Shift so the chain goes to the second largest. Then shift it back to the largest and check the alignment again.

15E-9. Now, if your arm hasn't fallen off from all that pedaling, shift to all five sprockets. Make sure it stays on each sprocket until you shift it off. Listen for the chain to be sure it's not hitting or rubbing on anything. Now get on the bike and give it a real test. Ain't it a honey?

Usually, you won't have to do all the adjusting—just the checking. However, if everything didn't go right, then we're faced with our old friend, the overhaul

In most cases, to remove the mounting bolt, you'll have to remove the rear wheel. (See Procedure 10F). You do recall that it's recommended that the chain be on the small front and rear sprockets for this.

15F-1. If you have the kind with the visible tension spring (Schwinn Approved, GT-100, Huret-Sprint, etc.), pry the spring up to relieve the tension. Otherwise, take the chain off the front sprocket.

15F-2. Before you disengage the chain from changer, make sure you see how it threads so you'll get it back the same way.

15F-3. Next, consult the exploded view of the typical rear changer (Figure 108). See the tension roller? Remove this by undoing the roller bolt. Make a note of the number and position of the washers for reassembly.

15F-4. Remove the cable and housing from the derailleur and then, by removing the mounting bolt, the entire unit comes off.

15F-5. Our typical rear derailleur is a Huret Allvit type. The same general disassembly procedures apply to Schwinn Approved, other than the GT-100. By holding the locknut, you can remove the jockey roller.

15F-6. This releases the two cage arms, the jockey roller (upper pulley), the tension springs and washers, spacers, and shims. (Different models may be different from the typical, so keep track.)

Chances are that if any part is damaged, it will be one of the two rollers or a spring. The other spring is the traverse or operating spring. If it or another part on the body is broken, go ahead and remove that part. Otherwise, clean it in solvent along with all the other parts except the plastic rollers. Some rollers will have hubs that come off to reveal bearings—always loose. Catch 'em, count 'em, and clean 'em. Check the balls for wear or pitting. If the plastic rollers are dirty, they will come clean with soap and water.

If any part needs replacement, take the old part along to be sure you get an exact replacement.

In putting it back together, be sure you get everything in the right order. And don't forget to line up the holes in the little washers with the hole in the derailleur body. That's where the tip of the tension spring goes.

Just reverse the order you used in disassembly, and when you get it back together, follow the adjustment procedure covered in Figures 109, 110, 111.

If you have a Simplex (Figure 112), follow the same steps in removing the unit.

15G-1. Then, using a proper-sized hex wrench, hold the main pivot bolt (that's the top one) while using an open end wrench to undo the rear locknut.

15G-2. Turn the hex counterclockwise to take the tension out.

15G-3. Now remove the locknut and pull out the pivot bolt.

15G-4. This will allow the upper traverse spring to come out of its shell.

15G-5. Move to the bottom of the unit. There is a stop on the cage at the top of the tension roller to keep the cage from rotating all the way around. Unscrew and remove this.

15G-6. Now, you've got a tension spring in the bottom. Loosen the locknut, hold onto it, and rotate the hex wrench counterclockwise to remove the tension.

15G-7. You can now spin the cage counterclockwise to unscrew and remove it from its pivot bolt.

15G-8. The pivot bolt will come off too when the locknut is removed, and this will expose the tension spring for removal.

15G-9. Back to the cage. Remove the roller bolts, making a note of the sequence of washers.

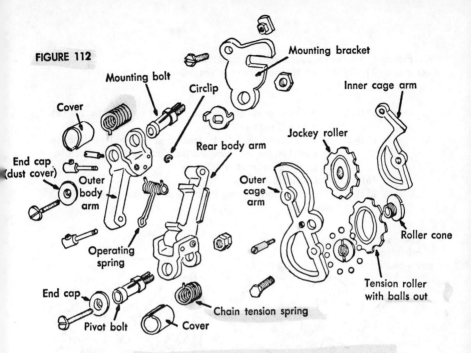

FIGURE 112

Mounting bracket
Mounting bolt
Circlip
Inner cage arm
Cover
Jockey roller
End cap (dust cover)
Rear body arm
Outer body arm
Outer cage arm
Roller cone
Operating spring
Tension roller with balls out
End cap
Chain tension spring
Pivot bolt
Cover

15G-10. The Simplex has a spring inside the body, as indicated in Figure 112. It has a pivot arm that keeps it in place. Unscrew this.

15G-11. If the rollers have removable hubs, take them off to get at the ball bearings—*loose*. Catch 'em, count 'em, and clean 'em.

Put all parts except the plastic rollers into solvent. On some models, the jockey roller is different from the tension roller. If so, make sure you can tell the difference at reassembly time.

Inspect all the clean parts for damage. The most likely suspect will be the rollers. Is the plastic damaged? Are the bearings worn or pitted? Are the cage arms bent? The next most common fault is in the springs. Check them over. See if any of the parts are worn, bent, scratched or pitted, or broken. Replace the bad guys. Use light oil on all the parts. In reassembly, the entire ritual is reversed. When it's all back together, follow all the adjustment procedures in 15E.

153

Figure 113 is an exploded view of a Campagnolo rear changer. Go through the same steps in removing the unit.

15H-1. If the cage pivot bolt is like the one shown, insert a hex wrench and remove.

15H-2. The cage end tip of the tension spring will be inserted in a hole in the outer cage arm. You'll want to remember which hole for reassembly.

15H-3. Disassemble the cage.

15H-4. The main body spring inside need not be removed if it's not broken.

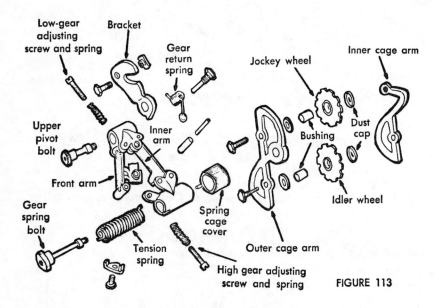

FIGURE 113

Put all parts except plastic rollers into solvent and clean them thoroughly. Inspect all parts. See that the rollers aren't damaged. Oil the roller bushings and reinsert them in the rollers. Check to be sure they turn easily. Look at the cage arms. Are they bent? Is the tension spring still OK? See if there are any bent, rusted, worn, or broken parts and replace any that are injured.

With everything shipshape, use light oil and reverse the procedure to put your Campagnolo back together. When the whole smear is back together and on the bike, go through the adjustment steps in 15E.

There are copies of each of the above derailleurs. Find the one nearest yours, and use that as a guide in overhauling.

Whatever kind you have, after it's back and adjusted, test it by riding it. If it's not 100 percent right, check it out again.

Front Derailleurs • If you have a 10-speed bike, you have a front derailleur unit that moves the chain from one front sprocket to another. They're all very much alike in principle, but some have one adjustment screw on top (Figure 114), and others have two (Figures 115 and 116). They both work on the parallelogram principle, established in 1840 by Pierre Parallelogram. The cable pulls the chain guide one way to move the chain from one sprocket to another, and the other way to move it back.

High

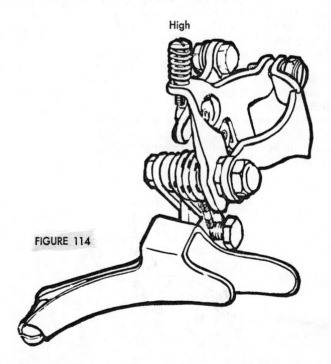

FIGURE 114

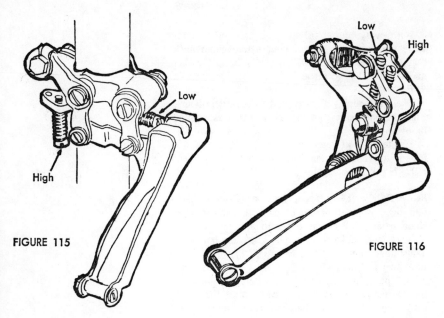

Low

High

FIGURE 115

Low

High

FIGURE 116

Usually, if it's faulty, it's out of adjustment. Try that first. The adjustment should be made starting with the chain on the smallest sprockets, front and back. Since you'll have to shift gears, be sure that the rear wheel is off the ground and that the pedals are moving forward when you shift. Check the cable, and if it has any slack, loosen the nut or screw anchoring the cable and pull the end tight. Anchor it back.

Now shift gears so the chain is on the big front sprocket. The chain guide should clear the large sprocket teeth by about ⅛ inch (as per the lines in Figure 117). If it doesn't, loosen the right tube

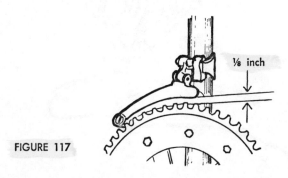

⅛ inch

FIGURE 117

clamp bolt and adjust. At the same time, make sure the arc of the chain guide is more or less parallel with the arc of the chainwheel.

Next, shift back so the chain goes back to the small front sprocket.

Now, all of you two-adjusting-screw folks need to put your screwdriver to the low-gear adjusting knobs. (One of the two two-screw models will be like yours—Figure 115 or 116.) Turn until the chain guide is exactly centered over the sprocket, and be sure the control lever has been pushed all the way. That accomplished, shift again to move the chain to the large sprocket and turn the high-gear adjusting screw to center the guide over the large sprocket.

If you're a one-adjusting-screw person, with the chain on the small front sprocket, there'll be a bolt holding the chain guide to the spindle. Loosen it. Move the guide until it's centered over the small sprocket. On some models, this also controls the attitude of the guide (Figure 118). At this time, make sure it's parallel to the chainwheel. Now shift so the chain moves to the big sprocket, and use your one adjusting screw to center the guide over the big sprocket.

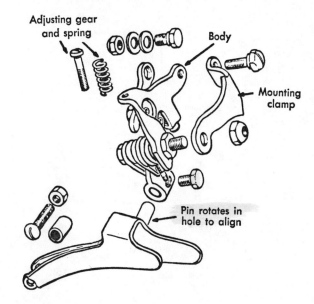

Adjusting gear and spring

Body

Mounting clamp

Pin rotates in hole to align

FIGURE 118

Either kind, turn the pedals and shift back and forth. If the chain rubs, adjust again.

If adjusting won't do it, you may have to dismantle, clean, and inspect the unit. It's a snap.

15I-1. Undo the cable anchor screw or nut and pull the cable out.

15I-2. Next, remove the small bolt at the bottom of the chain guide. Don't lose the nut or spacer!

15I-3. Remove the nuts, bolts, or screws that hold the clamp and unit to the seat tube. Keep tabs on all the small parts, as various units differ from the typical one in the exploded view.

Clean all parts in solvent and check for bent or broken parts, sprung springs (or is that *sprang?*), and stripped threads. Replace the bad guys.

In reinstalling, put the unit back together, and then clamp it to the tube. Easy does it on the tightness. Once it's back on, and the cable is attached, go through the adjustment routine we've already learned about.

That's about it for derailleurs. No matter what kind you have, by using the information here, plus your own brain, you'll be able to take it apart, see what's wrong, and put it back together. You can do it!

16
Accessories

You can add all sorts of things to your bike. In fact, you could add so much stuff to your machine that you wouldn't be able to move it. I've seen bikes where the accessories cost more than the bike itself. Here are a few thoughts about some popular add-ons.

_____ **Rear Derailleur Gears**

Get one! Either type shown will pay for itself the first time your bike falls over and the derailleur is protected (Figure 119).

FIGURE 119

Let there be light

Lights used for bikes are either battery powered or generator powered. Some battery-powered models are mounted on the bike, but some people install a holder in which a regular flashlight is slipped. This means your bike light can also be used for other things. It also means your bike light is never there when you need it.

Wrong way

There is also a battery-powered flashlight that straps to the rider's arm or leg. It has a pair of lenses pointed in opposite directions: one with clear glass, and the other with red. This gives you a headlight and taillight all in one—it still is usually somewhere else when you need it.

The generator type gets its power when a groovy wheel (shown in Figure 120) is placed against a moving tire. By the way, this wheel is known as a *pulley* in the bike game. The turning wheel turns the pulley which turns the insides of the generator, which causes the lights attached to glow. (Incidentally, the generator is referred to as a *dynamo* in the bike game.) Some systems have only a headlight, while others have both front and rear lights. The disadvantage of this type is that you have to be moving to be seen.

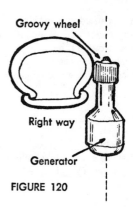

Groovy wheel

Right way

Generator

FIGURE 120

From an installation standpoint, the instructions will be included when you buy the unit. The only two things to be careful of are the positioning of the generator with regard to the way the pulley rides against the tire and the positioning of the generator with regard to the axis of the wheel. Figure 120 shows the right and the wrong way for the pulley to touch the tire. Figure 121 shows how the unit should line up with the axis—for either front or back wheel.

Maintenance is simple on light systems. Burned-out bulbs should be replaced. Carry spares in a plastic sandwich bag inside the handlebars. Battery models need new batteries when the lights start to get dim, not when they go completely out. Generator pulleys begin to lose their grooves and should be replaced. Wires can become frayed or come loose, so check them at the first failure.

FIGURE 121

How fast and how far

Lots of cyclers want to know how fast they are going and how far they have been. Personally, the feeling of speed is more important to me than my exact miles per hour. And if I know that I've been going for nine miles, I'm liable to start thinking it's about time to get tired, so I've removed those gadgets from my bike. If you want this information, however, it is easy to install either a speedometer for how fast, or a cyclometer for how far. (Usually, the bike speedometer will also tell how far.)

The only thing you have to know in buying one is the wheel size. The gadget will be calibrated for a particular wheel size, and if not on the right-size wheel will give inaccurate readings. Each unit will have easy-to-follow instructions.

Bells and Horns

I have mixed emotions about signaling devices for bikes. Some states require some sort. Most bike horns aren't loud enough for a motorist to hear—particularly if he's got the windows closed with the heater or the air-conditioner going and is listening to the radio. The kind that will get through all that noise is the air horn. This baby has a replaceable aerosol can of Freon and can be heard a mile away. It also gives pedestrians heart seizures. It's also very attractive to thieves. A guy who wouldn't think of stealing your bike would see lots of fun ahead with an air horn.

The horns with squeeze bulbs that are big enough to be heard require you to let go of the handlebar with one hand to squeeze. Usually, that's about the time you need both hands.

Electric horns are in between in decibels. The button can be positioned on the handlebar so you can still steer while you honk. Some motorists can hear them, and only the frailest of pedestrians will have heart attacks.

161

Bottles

The in thing even for riding around the neighborhood is to have a bottle carrier mounted on the seat tube. There's a plastic thermal bottle that will keep martinis cold for hours. Actually, they're called feeder bottles. If it weren't for the fact that I carry martinis in case of snake bite, I wouldn't have one.

Pumps

A tube mount pump is a good thing to have if you get very far afield. Be sure to get the kind that fits your valves. Hand pumping is hard work, but riding on soft tires can ruin them.

A bicycle pump often quits putting out air because the leather washer inside dries out. It no longer seals against the cylinder. This is really a simple matter to take care of. By saturating the washer with oil, it will expand, and usually make the pump function again. If that was what was wrong with your pump, remember to give the washer a shot of lubricant every six months or so to keep it from drying out again.

Tire-Protecting Nail Catchers

If you have tubular tires with a thread pattern that runs around the tire—not across—you might want a set of nail catchers. They are easily attached to the mounting post of both front and rear caliper brakes. The one in Figure 122 is typical. The gadget lightly brushes the tire as it rotates to whisk away nails or other sharp objects before they cause a puncture. I'm not all shook up over these, but some people swear by them. It's up to you!

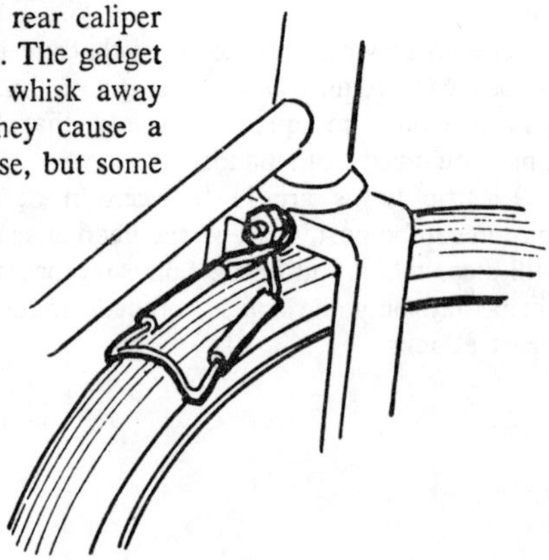

FIGURE 122

Training Wheels

Shown here are typical training wheels (Figure 123). These are an aid to the brand new cycler. The alternative is to have someone run alongside to keep the new rider from losing balance. Unless you have several other riders coming up, you'll spend three to eight dollars for training wheels that will be used for about three to eight days. Scout the neighborhood and see if there isn't a set you can borrow or buy for a buck.

FIGURE 123

Fenders (Mudguards)

Time was when all the classier jobs had chrome fenders. Now, many of the bikes that cost three or four hundred dollars don't come with fenders, and their owners wouldn't let you put them on if you paid them. However, if you have fenders, rejoice in the fact that there is a strong fender cult throughout the world. If you have fenders and want to strip them off, or if you have fenders and need to take them off for other repairs, here's your guide:

The front wheel will probably have to come off before you can get to the nut that attaches the fender to the fork. Figure 124 shows a typical hidden-by-the-tire nut. If there is a nut on the back of the fork as shown in Figure 125, then you're in luck— the wheel can stay on. Next, there are probably a pair of fender braces (Figure 124). Either screws or nuts will hold these.

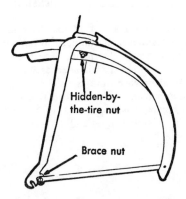

Hidden-by-the-tire nut

Brace nut

FIGURE 124

The back wheel may also have to come off. We found out in Chapter 10 that this is a little bit more complicated than removing the front wheel. Check to see whether there is a back stay clip like this—if so, the fender can probably be removed by undoing the bolt through this and nuts or screws on the fender braces. If the hardware is located on the inside of the fender, sit down and try to talk yourself out of removing it. (Don't be surprised if the man at the bike shop refers to your fenders as mudguards).

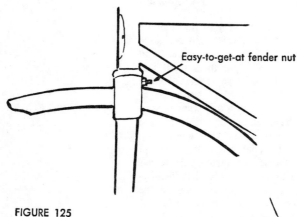

Easy-to-get-at fender nut

FIGURE 125

Kickstands

Most bikes come with a kickstand that lasts for the life of the bike. However, if you need to replace yours, most of them are similar to the type shown (Figure 126). You can see that it attaches on the side opposite the chainwheel and is held on by a bolt through the top plate. The only two things to be careful of in buying a new one are (1) be sure the top plate will fit your frame; and (2) get one made for your size bike.

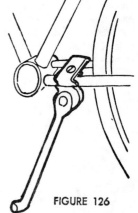

FIGURE 126

There are also kickstands that come straight down, called *V* stands. The picture is from memory because I have never had one and couldn't find anybody in the neighborhood with one (Figure 127).

Speaking of memory, here is the kind of stand I had as a kid. When in place, it lifted the rear wheel off the ground so you could get your pedaling exercise in the house with just the back wheel spinning around. Every once in a while, the movement would jar the bike so it came off the stand and sent you and the bike burning rubber right through the Oriental screen.

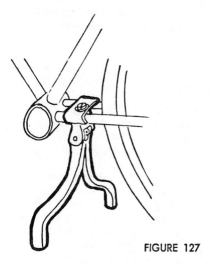

FIGURE 127

17

Special Bikes

Since we left the section on the history of the machine, we haven't mentioned much except the conventional bicycle. There are some noteworthy specialty-type vehicles.

_____ **Tandems**

The most popular specialty is the bicycle built for two. Several major manufacturers have a tandem bike in their line. This is a fun machine for couples, providing of course that both partners are willing to do their share.

If you've moved up to a 10-speed and have a couple of old bikes in the garage, it's possible you might want to tackle the project of converting two regular bikes into a tandem. There will have to be adjustments for different types of bikes, but this basic plan will give you the general idea. If you don't have the skill, desire, tools, or time to enter into this conversion, take the book and your two bikes to that friendly old bike repairman and see if he wouldn't like to get in on the fun. I priced such a project and found the estimates ran from $23.50 to $80.00. The bike man will end up with some spare parts which are worth something to him, and he will have to put very little into the conversion other than his time. But why not do it yourself?

The first step is to join the two frames. The

diagram shows the use of a pair of boys' bikes, but one or both could just as easily have been the open-frame girl's-type bike. The dotted lines show what should be removed from each machine (Figure 128).

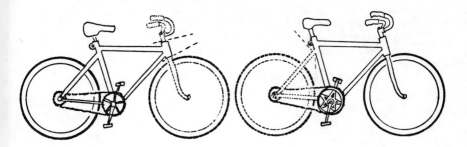

FIGURE 128

The method of joining could have been a weld instead of the nuts and bolts. Probably the best way to decide just how you're going to put the two together is to stand them next to each other with the front wheel of one even with the back wheel of the other. This will give you an idea of how they will match up, and thus, how the frames can be joined.* Next, give the parts you won't need the dotted line treatment as I did in the drawing.

If the headset column of the rear bike is too long for the seat post of the leader, there are two ways to go: (1) cut it down—a not-too-much-fun task; or (2) get a longer seat post.

You may even decide to cut this part off and join the two frames by leaving about as much of the frame of the front bike up there as we've left down by the sprocket. This would give a surface on which to weld or bolt the top and down tubes of the rear cycle. This is probably not going to be that easy, since the tubes will have to be bent some to get it all together.

* Be sure that your plan will allow the finished frame to be such that the pedals will be well up off the surface. If possible, do not lower their position at all.

Let's say it all fits the way it does in the drawing. The headset column must be fixed to the seat post (Figure 129). If you don't have a welding rig, drill a pair of holes all the way through and secure the parts with nuts and bolts. Since the seat should never be raised or lowered, take this into consideration when making the connection. Then it would be a good idea to drill through the frame of the front bike and bolt the seat post in position. Be sure to remember the rule of thumb for seat posts:

> RULE OF THUMB: *Seat posts must always have at least 2½ inches inside the frame.*

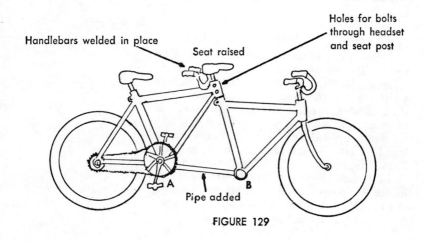

Handlebars welded in place

Seat raised

Holes for bolts through headset and seat post

A

Pipe added

B

FIGURE 129

Now you need a support pipe from point *A* to point *B*. A scrap of pipe must be cut to fit, and try to find one that is about the same diameter as the frame. It'll look better. (Here again, you may wish to weld instead of bolt.)

Now comes the last part of rigging the frame—the attaching of the rear handlebars. These are to be stationary—merely for gripping, not for steering. As you can see, my plan calls for the handlebars to be welded to the corner formed by the frame top tube and the headset column. This decision came after I looked through my various junk drawers for a gadget like the one shown. I remember removing one from something that looked a lot like this (Figure 130), but I couldn't find it. Some bike stems have a clamp for the handlebars that is movable, and this would be ideal. However, the bike shops would only sell the entire stem assembly, and I wasn't able to find a junked part. So, I welded.

Now, if you can apply a slick paint job, the frame is finished and should look pretty good.

Now comes the hard part. You now have to provide the rear unit with a dual chainwheel. The chain from the lead bike has to go around one chainwheel, and the chain from the rear unit goes to the rear sprocket to provide the go-power. Figure 131 sure looks simple enough, doesn't it? One of the hard parts is that you will now have to spend a little loot. You'll need a chainwheel, and this will run from two to five dollars. A used one will do just fine if you can find one. Just make sure the chain from the front bike fits the teeth of the new chainwheel. The two are joined by inserting bolts in the holes you have drilled on each sprocket. There has to be room between for the chains, so you'll need to add spacers.

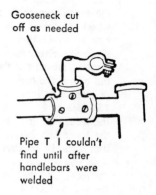

Gooseneck cut off as needed

Pipe T I couldn't find until after handlebars were welded

FIGURE 130

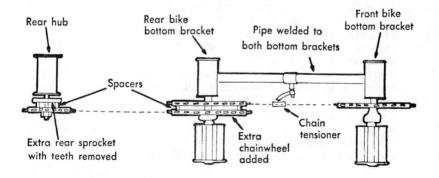

Rear hub

Rear bike bottom bracket

Pipe welded to both bottom brackets

Front bike bottom bracket

Spacers

Extra rear sprocket with teeth removed

Extra chainwheel added

Chain tensioner

FIGURE 131

The outer chainwheel has to be adapted to allow the crank arm to fit tight against the inner chainwheel. This may be a simple task or a difficult one, but it can be done. The spacers have moved the chain to the rear sprocket out, and the rear sprocket must be moved out the same distance. Probably the old bike is the coaster type, and if you're lucky, the rear sprocket looks like the one pictured in Figure 132. See how it is offset? By reversing it, it moves the teeth out, and yet will still fit back in place on the inner hub barrel. Hope it's like that one, and that it can be set over far enough to line up. Otherwise, you will have to buy a second sprocket, remove the teeth, add the proper spacers between, and join the two to form a gadget that looks like the one in Figure 131.

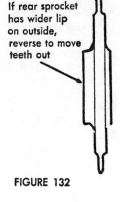

If rear sprocket has wider lip on outside, reverse to move teeth out

FIGURE 132

Now all you need for proper adjustment of the chains is a little gadget called a chain tensioner for the front chain. By the time I got this far, I had all sorts of pressure to finish, and so I bought a regular tensioner at a bike shop. It's made for store-bought tandems and is attached as shown.

Now you are ready to roll and sing the old "Daisy, Daisy, give me your answer . . ." Maybe you'd better save your breath for those hills because you know your partner is going to ease up and let you do all the work.

Trike Bikes

The three-wheeler bicycles are ideal for the person who wants the exercise and mobility of a bike, but doesn't want to worry about having to keep balanced. They come in 1- and 3-speed. Be sure to get one with a parking brake.

For the tinkerer, there is a conversion kit on the market that will change a two-wheeled bike into a three-wheeler. It's for 1-, 2-, and 3-speed bikes. I've never converted a bike with this kind of kit, but it looks easy enough.

Your bike dealer probably won't have one in stock, but he'll know where to order it. Be sure that you order for your size bike and that it will work for your kind of gears.

Unicycles

I was going to write a long piece on this machine until I broke my left-hand typing finger trying to learn to ride one. Shown here is the plan I used to make it from an old tricycle front wheel (Figure 133)

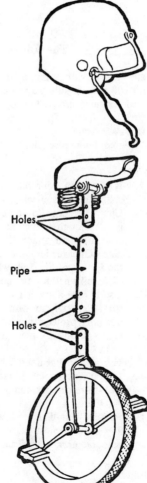

Holes

Pipe

Holes

Holes drilled so three parts can be bolted together

FIGURE 133

18

Security, Storage, and Hauling

--------------------- **The Bicycle Thief**

Bikes do get stolen and with alarming regularity. Maybe there's no 100 percent sure way to keep your bike safe from a determined crook, but most crooks don't want to work very hard. After all, they usually steal to keep from working.

Here are a few commonsense rules to protect your bike:

18A-1. Never leave your bike unlocked. Many people lock and chain them even when they bring them inside.

18A-2. Chain the bike to something sturdy and something that is tall enough so the chain can't be lifted over it. Also, be sure that you attach the chain to a sturdy part of your bike. One reader who used to loop the chain through the spokes of his front wheel returned to find that the rest of the bike had been removed.

18A-3. Use a case-hardened alloy steel chain or stranded cable sturdy enough to withstand an assault. Plastic covering not only protects the finish on your bike but also deters chain cutting. A new plastic fused with fibers will soon be out.

18A-4. Use a lock that doesn't have many keys that fit it.

18A-5. If you have a combination lock that can be set, avoid easy-to-remember combinations such as 0, 0, 0; 1, 2, 3; 7–11, etc.

18A-6. Record your bike serial number, even though it won't do any good in most cases other than as identification. Most manufacturers and dealers don't record the numbers. Repair shops don't check the number to see if it's "hot" when a bike is brought in. If your local police department has a bike registration setup, use it. Ask about it!

18A-7. An electric etching tool can be used to mark the under-side of a lot of the parts on your bike.

18A-8. Find out if your bike is covered by your homeowner's policy. If not, get coverage.

18A-9. Learn to think like a thief—and outfox him.

Storage

We mentioned the importance of bringing your bike inside to foil the thief. It's also important to protect your bike from Mother Nature. (No, she's not the head of a ring of bike rustlers.)

The garage, basement, or tool shed is a logical place to store your bike—unless these spots get damp in rainy weather. Many riders bring their bikes right inside the house. If you keep your bike clean, there's no reason why it can't be in with you. If stairs are a problem in getting your bike in and out, here's a hint recently sent in by a reader:

"Rather than leave my bike outside for someone to 'borrow,' I bring it up the front steps and leave it in our guest closet. I soon found out that bouncing it up and down the steps was not the easiest thing on me or the wheels. Then I created a ramp that allows me to roll it up and down with very little effort. I cut a board to span the steps and put pieces on each side to form a U-shaped channel. This keeps the wheels on the track. When not in use, the ramp is put against the wall on the porch and is completely out of the way.

"Really a groovy idea for anyone who has had to struggle up and down steps with a bike. Make the groove out of fairly lightweight wood so it will be easy to position."

Many riders put their bikes away for the winter. Those less hardy souls* find a screw hook to be about the greatest thing going. One strategically

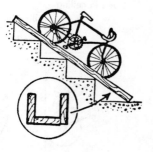

FIGURE 134

* EDITOR'S NOTE: The author refers to less hardy souls putting their bikes away for the winter when he lives in a clime that has no winter.

placed screw hook in a garage or a basement ceiling will allow a bike to hang down with the wheels against the wall, as shown in Figure 135. Vinyl-coated screw hooks are preferable because bare metal could mar your wheel. If you buy the unclad kind at the hardware store, slip a section of rubber tubing over the hook. There are other ways to use the hooks, as we have shown.

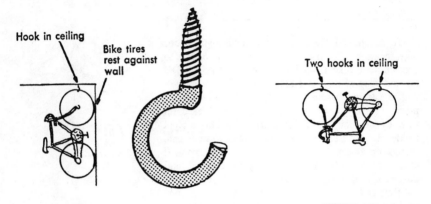

FIGURE 135

Shelf braces are also good wall hangers. Position them up on the wall at the desired height so they support the top tube if it's a man's bike. If it's a gal's model, position the back brace under the seat stay. So as not to scratch the frame, glue a strip of foam rubber along the brace. The strap across the top is a good precaution to prevent the bike from accidentally being knocked off on someone's head.

Old leather belts can be attached to the garage wall to form straps for bike parking. Form one loop for the handlebar to fit through, then position a belt with buckle to go around the seat post. This will keep the bike upright and against the wall where it will be out of the way.

174

Here's a bike rack from my previous book, *Super Handyman's Encyclopedia of Home Repair Hints*, also published by Prentice-Hall. This was sent in by one of my readers:

"Let me tell you about the bicycle rack I made from an old metal bedstead that has upright end pieces every 6 inches or so. By removing the casters and setting the legs in cement, we had a rack that was as good as the ones in the school yard. With the front wheel stuck between the uprights, the children also lock the bikes to the rack at night."

————————————— Hauling your bike

As promised, we want you to know some of the ways to haul your bike in, on, or around your car

There are a number of good trunk and rear bumper racks on the market. Bike shops, department stores, mail-order houses, and automotive supply houses will usually carry one or more styles. They are easy to install and easy to remove—in most cases. When buying a rack, make sure you get one that will fit your kind of car. Even a type that clamps on a bug's back is available.

There are also rooftop carriers. Some of these will carry as many as four bicycles. Just remember you've got extra height, so look out for low limbs and bridges.

If you are handy at making things, you can fashion your own carrier. Take a look at some of the ready-made jobs and you will see that they are fairly simple in design. (Pricing them may spur you into action to do-it-yourself.)

Whether you buy or make an auto bike carrier rack, I'd strongly suggest you try to have one that allows you to lock the bike to the rack and the rack to the car if it's to be left unattended.

Hauling it in the trunk • If you have to, many cars have room enough for you to haul your bicycle in the trunk. This depends on the kind of car. Most of the time you'll have to remove the front wheel and the handlebars.

175

Incidentally, if you have a road failure and have to call a friend to come get you and your bike, ask him to bring tools to do this. Otherwise, you may end up having to tie the lid down or not having ample rear vision or both.

RULE OF THUMB: *Don't call a friend with a Volkswagen.*

If you get so hooked on cycling that you want to take touring or camping trips on your bike, you will find it a real pleasure.

I'd suggest you find the nearest bicycle club. Its members are probably doing the touring and camping bit on a regular basis. If they turn out to be your kind of people, you might find joining the club will get you off to a quick start on these new adventures. You will probably be taking advantage of the previous experiences of a lot of other cyclers.

Many people take their bikes along on vacations. Most airlines have provisions for shipping bicycles. Just be sure to check all the airlines you'll be using on the trip, as they differ in their rules.

Another way to cycle after you get to the vacation spot is to find a rental agency. Don't expect the rented bike to handle as well as your own. Do insist on at least getting one to fit and adjusting the seat and handlebars for your comfort and safety.

Maybe after reading this book and working on your bike, you'll be able to completely dismantle it, put it in a sack—and then put it back together when you get there.

Index